Books by James Jespersen & Jane Fitz-Randolph

TIME AND CLOCKS FOR THE SPACE AGE

MERCURY'S WEB

RAMS, ROMS AND ROBOTS

FROM QUARKS TO QUASARS

From Quarks to Quasars

A Tour of the Universe

FROM QU

TO

A TOUR OF T

by James Jespersen

Illustrated with diagrams by Bruce Hiscock

ATHENEUM

ARKS

QUASARS

HE UNIVERSE

& Jane Fitz-Randolph

and with prints and photographs

NEW YORK 1987

Atheneum
Macmillan Publishing Company
866 Third Avenue, New York, NY 10022
Composition by Arcata Graphics/Kingsport, Kingsport, Tennessee
Printed & bound by R. R. Donnelley & Sons, Harrisonburg, Virginia
Designed by Mary Ahern
First Edition
10 9 8 7 6 5 4 3 2 1

Library of Congress Cataloging-in-Publication Data

Jespersen, James.   From quarks to quasars.

Includes index.
SUMMARY: *Discusses the theories advanced over the past several*
hundred years explaining the nature of the universe.
1. Cosmology—Juvenile literature.   2. Nuclear physics—Juvenile
literature.   3. Astrophysics—Juvenile literature.
[1. Cosmology.   2. Nuclear physics.
3. Astrophysics] I. Fitz-Randolph, Jane.   II. Title.
QB983.J47   1987   523.1   86–17276
ISBN 0–689–31270–9

For
Sherry, Ted, Cliff and Jim

Contents

From Quarks to Quasars

A Tour of the Universe

1

Of Kangaroos and Other Things

WHAT SOUNDS do ocean waves make? How does it feel to go whizzing down a mountain slope on skis? What does an avocado taste like? How does coffee smell? Describing something, even something quite familiar, to someone who has never experienced it is always hard. Suppose you are asked to describe a kangaroo to someone who has never seen one or heard of such an animal.

"Well," you begin, "it has four legs, but it walks on its hind legs, which are much larger and longer than the front ones. On second thought, it doesn't really walk; it jumps. It also has a long tail which it uses with its back legs to steady itself, something like a camera tripod. And the mother carries her baby in a pouch on her stomach. . . ."

Even if your friend gets a vague idea of a kangaroo from your description, it sounds like such an improbable animal that he may suspect you are pulling his leg. Trying to describe the universe, from the smallest particle to the largest galaxy, is much like trying to describe a kangaroo. The underlying nature of the universe is so far removed from our everyday experiences that it's hard to portray and to understand the picture modern science has painted. Yet the story of how this picture has unfolded is as fascinating as any science-fiction story and as challenging to our imagination and capacity for abstract thinking.

Part of the problem is that we try to understand new concepts in terms of the ones we feel comfortable with, just as we describe a kangaroo in terms of legs, tail, and pouch. But the fact is that a kangaroo is a unique animal which eventually must be understood on its own terms rather than as some Tinkertoy version built from parts of other, more familiar animals.

Another part of the problem is that in exploring the universe we are dealing with objects that are often much smaller or much larger than we can comprehend. The kangaroo at least falls well within normal limits of animal sizes. In everyday life we are used to dealing with objects ranging from specks of dust, marbles, and basketballs to automobiles, steamships, and icebergs. Much beyond either end of this size scale we lose a sense of what is being described, and what makes the description even harder is that the smallest and largest objects in the universe don't behave like marbles and icebergs; they behave in ways that seem just as improbable as the existence and behavior of a kangaroo.

Scientists have long used mathematics to overcome the limitations of everyday language. Verbal theories cannot be made exact enough to test which one is closest to being "truth." With mathematics, scientists can communicate their ideas precisely to other scientists. Unfortunately, though, the abstract mathematics used in physical theories is not readily understandable by people who have not devoted a good deal of time and effort to the study of physics, astronomy, mathematics, and other scientific subjects. Yet science and technology, although often nearly invisible, are an important part of modern life; so trying to understand the flavor of modern science, even though we haven't the time or interest to probe nature with the dedication of a professional scientist, is well worth our effort.

Fortunately, we don't have to know the details to understand the goals and methods of science, just as we don't need to know all the rules of a football game—as a football official must—to enjoy the game. We don't have to be concert violinists to appreciate a symphony.

One of the most famous figures of modern science is the Danish physicist Niels Bohr. It was Professor Bohr who put on a scientific basis, the idea that the atom is something like a miniature solar system, with a central nucleus circled by one or more electrons. And in this analogy we see another example of explaining something unfamiliar—an atom—in terms of the more familiar—the solar system.

Bohr was well known for his dry sense of humor as well as his hospitality. In the 1920s and 1930s he headed an institute for theoretical physics in Denmark, which was supported by the Carlsberg Brewery. Bohr often invited visiting scientists to his home for dinner. On one such occasion a nervous young scientist from the United States who had received one of the coveted invitations stood at the Bohr threshold waiting for the door to open in response to his knock. As he waited, he noticed a horseshoe nailed above the door. This surprised him because he could not imagine that Professor Bohr would believe in such a talisman.

After dinner, when Bohr and the young scientist were sitting in the Bohr family library discussing mutual interests, the young scientist finally mustered enough courage to mention the horseshoe and ask Bohr if he really believed that horseshoes bring good luck.

"Of course not," said Bohr. He paused, then added, "But I understand they work even if you don't believe in them."

Modern science is a lot like Bohr's horseshoe. The theories are so far removed from everyday experience that they seem unreal; yet they work exceedingly well whether we believe in them or not.

The history of progress in science has been one of gathering apparently unrelated phenomena under the same umbrella of explanation. The familiar story of Sir Isaac Newton and the apple tree is a good example. Newton, according to the story, was sitting under an apple tree when he saw an apple fall to the ground, and he began speculating about why it fell. This incident allegedly gave him the idea for his universal law of gravitation.

What was it that clicked in Newton's mind? He realized that the force that governed the apple's fall was the same force that governs the planetary and lunar motions. Before Newton's extraordinary idea, it was not apparent that falling apples had anything to do with the moon orbiting the earth. Here is a clear case of combining earthbound motion with celestial motion under the umbrella of universal gravitation.

Since Newton's time scientists have discovered other forces. One is the electromagnetic force, which was at one time thought to be two separate forces. The mysterious, invisible magnetic force that caused the visible fluctuations of a compass needle was thought to be distinct from the electric force that causes bits of paper to cling to a hard-rubber comb passed through the hair, but the Scottish mathematical physicist James Clerk Maxwell was able to show in the last century that electricity and magnetism are really two aspects of a single force—the electromagnetic force. And again we see two apparently unrelated phenomena brought together.

In our century scientists have discovered two more forces—the *weak* force and the *strong* force. As we shall see, these forces are related to atomic phenomena and so were not discovered until scientists began to probe the nature of the atom. But now, just in the last decade, the weak force has been joined with the electromagnetic force. In 1984 two scientists, Carlo Rubbia and Simon van der Meer, working at the CERN laboratories in Geneva, Switzerland, received a Nobel prize for verifying the unified weak-electromagnetic force. And before this, in 1979, the scientific community had been so sure of the unified weak-electromagnetic force that, even though no experiment had yet confirmed it convincingly, three other scientists were awarded a Nobel Prize for proposing it.

Today the search is on for one grand theory to unify gravity, the weak-electromagnetic force, and the strong force. And so we see, without knowing any of the mathematical details, that one of the goals of science is to gather as many phenomena as possible into the fewest number of theories, but the price we pay for this unification is theories that are far removed from human experience.

The unification that science seeks is not arbitrary, however. At any one time there are usually many theories competing to explain some new observation; quite often several of the theories adequately account for the observation. So which theory is correct? Well, until some observation provides a reason to choose one over the others, we have to say that all are correct. But science does not leave the matter there. The normal course is to pick the theory that explains the most with the least. This seems reasonable enough. Why work with a cumbersome theory when a simpler one makes the correct prediction?

Although looking for the simplest theory that will do the job is a very important principle of modern science, it is not new. The idea seems to have been spelled out first by William of Ockham, who was born in Ockham, in the county of Surrey in England, about 1285. William was a very practical, down-to-earth man who did not trust abstract ideas. He did not believe in the Greek philosopher Plato's notion that the only "true realities" were ideal versions of their imperfect earthly representations. Plato believed, for example, that a circle drawn with a compass by the human hand is just a "shadow" of some "real" circle that exists only as an idea.

William believed that objects that could not be seen were not real. The people who subscribed to Plato's theory, the universalists, concocted ever more complex theories to support their position—a practice that annoyed William. Finally, in frustration, he laid down a rule: "Entities must not needlessly be multiplied." In other words, Don't make something unnecessarily complicated. As we shall see,

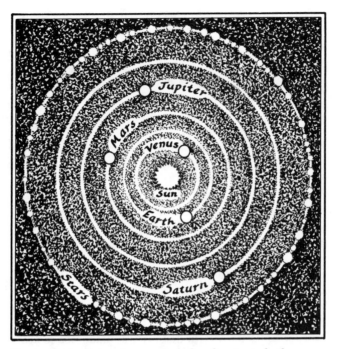

Fig. 1. In the Copernican system, the planets circle the sun, and the outermost orbit contains the stars.

this simple principle will be one of our most useful guideposts in our tour of the universe.

Sometimes it is not easy, though, because of political, religious, or other reasons, to follow William's simple rule, or *Ockham's razor* as it is called today. The Egyptian astronomer Ptolemy had proposed around 150 A.D. that the earth stood at the center of the universe, with the moon and the planets revolving around the earth. To account for the motions of the celestial bodies in this system, it is necessary to assume that they move in complex orbits that Ptolemy called epicycles. Although the theory was complex, it did predict the lunar and planetary motions well enough to account for naked-eye observations.

Some thirteen hundred years later, Copernicus, the Polish founder of modern astronomy, proposed that if one assumed the sun, not the earth, as the center of the universe, the chore of predicting celestial motions was greatly reduced. With this change, the complicated planetary motions disappeared and were replaced by motions in circular orbits (fig. 1).

In 1512 Copernicus began to work out a detailed mathematical version of his theory, but these details were not published until 1543, the year he died. The reason for the long delay was that Copernicus feared that the heretical notion that the sun, not the earth, was the center of the universe would get him into trouble. The Roman Catholic church was very powerful at that time, and the church believed that the earth, being the home of man, God's special creation, should be the center of the universe. Copernicus could have been imprisoned for advancing his idea. Although using the Copernican scheme was not prohibited, since it made the calculations easier, practically all educated people believed that the earth was truly the center of the universe.

Still the matter was not so simple because the Copernican theory not only made the calculations easier, but it also cleared up some problems that plagued Ptolemy's theory. One particularly vexing problem had to do with the motion of the planet Venus. As we know now, Venus moves around the sun in an ellipse inside the earth's orbit. Accounting for Venus's orbit in Ptolemy's scheme required an enormously complex movement that in a way amounted to no explanation at all. In any case, because the Copernican theory reduced computational complexity and disposed of some problems, it was very tempting to suggest that the sun, not the earth, was indeed the center of the universe.

When Copernicus's book came out in 1543, several weeks after his death, it contained an unauthorized preface by a Lutheran minister, Andreas Osiander, who stated that the Copernican theory was not proposed as a factual representation of planetary motion but simply as a device to ease the chore of computing planetary motion. But even with this caution the book was banned by the Roman Catholic church until 1835.

Although he was greatly influenced by Greek thought, Copernicus as much as anyone else started man on the road to modern science and away from Greek science, which was based more on authority than on experiment. It is doubtful that Copernicus knew of Ockham's razor; but as we shall see, time and again simplicity and economy, in one way or another, have been underlying themes in all of modern science. And yet this seemingly obvious principle has led further and further away from the common sense view of things. After all, what could be more obvious to the naked eye than that the earth is the unmoving center of the universe?

But this denial of common sense, the Copernican theory under-written by Ockham's razor, was an invitation to a new view of the world—a view where the concrete visible was gradually replaced by the abstract invisible. It became increasingly clear that common sense, a useful guide in everyday life, was not a trustworthy tool for understanding the universe.

Next we shall explore another guiding principle of modern science—a principle developed over a thousand years before Ockham's razor by the Greeks, who had, above almost all other values, a passion for symmetry.

2

Elephants All the Way

P R O G R E S S in science is often the outgrowth of confusion and misunderstanding. Alexander Graham Bell's invention of the telephone resulted from his belief that he was repeating what had been done earlier by the German scientist Hermann von Helmholtz. Helmholtz had described, in German, a device he had constructed to reproduce vowel sounds. But Bell, because of his poor understanding of German, thought Helmholtz was describing a telephone-like device.

Much earlier, in 1492, Columbus had sailed westward from Spain believing that he would reach India. He had discarded the generally accepted belief that the earth was flat, in favor of a spherical earth, but he had made an erroneous estimate of its size; he thought it much smaller than it is—or at least he persuaded his backers that it was smaller. There is some speculation that he deliberately underestimated the size to attract investors. In any case, his error led to discovery of the New World.

We know from many notes written in the margins of books from Columbus's library that he had depended heavily on the work of Ptolemy for his estimate of the earth's size and shape. Ptolemy's estimate was based largely on the work of others—earlier Greek and Egyptian geographers who came amazingly close to determining the earth's actual circumference by measuring the length of shadows cast by the sun at different latitudes on the same day.

But even earlier Greek scholars, in the fifth century B.C., believed the earth was a sphere, for esthetic rather than observational reasons. After all, they argued, the sphere is the perfect shape, so of course it stands to reason that the earth would be a spheroid.

10

Some 150 years later, Aristotle, who was Plato's pupil, agreed, and he added some arguments of his own. He reasoned that the earth, standing at the center of the universe, would be a sphere because "bodies" falling toward the center from all sides would form a sphere. In the Greek system a second sphere, centered on and surrounding the earth, revolved around the earth; the second sphere carried the sun and stars.

Later Greek and Egyptian geographers had their own reasons for believing the earth was a sphere. One of the most convincing had to do with lunar eclipses. It was well known to Greek and Egyptian astronomers by 200 B.C. that the earth blocked sunlight from reaching the moon during a lunar eclipse. Put a little differently, the shadow on the moon was the shadow of the earth, and that shadow had to follow the earth's shape. Anyone who has watched a lunar eclipse knows that the earth is curved, not square or box-shaped, as some persons have supposed even into this century.

But refusal to give up an outgrown idea for a new one that works better often creates paradoxes with no answers. Unwillingness to exchange a flat earth for a spherical one, for example, created insolvable problems. If the earth is flat, we are left with the problem of whether it is bounded or has infinite extent. If it is bounded, would we fall off the edge? And fall to where? But on the other hand, it is difficult to believe in a world of infinite extent. What we need is a world that is bounded but has no edges. Impossible? No, not if the world is a sphere. But having removed one set of paradoxes by going from a flat earth to a spherical one, we create a new paradox: What holds the earth up?

Greek mythology proposed that a Titan named Atlas supported the earth and the heavens on his shoulders, and some myths from India propose that the earth rested on the back of an elephant. The next natural question is, what supports the elephant? One Indian mystic, questioned on this point, said that the elephant stood on the back of another elephant, and when asked what supported the second elephant, he replied that it was simply "elephants all the way."

Although a spherical earth was a cornerstone of Greek science, the belief came under heavy fire as faith replaced evidence under the Roman Catholic church. As early as 300 A.D., Lactantius, the Christian tutor to the Emperor Constantine's son, said, "Can anyone be so foolish as to believe that there are men whose feet are higher than their heads, or places where things may be hanging downwards?"

In some Indian mythologies,
the world rests on the back of an elephant.

The church was at odds with a spherical earth for several reasons. One of the most important had to do with the notion of "antipodes"— literally, "the place where men's feet are opposite." According to the theory of antipodes, there was an uncrossable band of fire ringing the earth at the equator, separating the earth into two halves. This meant that there was a group of people on the other side of the antipode who were forever isolated from the teachings of the church and therefore from redemption. The easiest way to solve this problem was to say the earth was not a sphere, thereby at one stroke abolishing the possibility of the existence of the antipodes.

Although this solution may sound ridiculous to us, it is perhaps no more ridiculous than insisting, as did the Greeks, that all celestial motions must be in circles. Science does not develop in a vacuum, but is at every stage conditioned by cultural, religious, and political values. Human beings—scientists included—have a strong tendency to want things to stay the way they are, or at least the way they have come to understand and accept them. Given new evidence, it is often just as difficult to modify scientific theories because of long-held human values as it is because of long-held scientific beliefs.

Still, little by little—or sometimes in great leaps—our understanding of nature's laws *has* changed and grown. Although Lactantius was disturbed by the idea of "things hanging downwards," the concept of a spherical earth does not bother anyone today, and we do not find it difficult to understand. Atoms and molecules are fairly familiar to us, but a universe that includes black holes and quasars, matter and antimatter, quarks and leptons still seems far out.

So it has always been. New theories grow out of old ones, and without the old ones to ponder and take apart, the philosophers and scientists of each period would probably not have come up with the new theories they introduced. Similarly, if *we* are to understand and appreciate the present concepts of the universe, we too need to follow through the steps taken by many different scientists, from many different countries and cultures, that have led to the picture of the universe as it appears today.

More than a thousand years after all these early theories and conjectures, the idea of simplicity and the Greek passion for symmetry, or balance, strongly influenced Copernicus in at least two ways—one of them good, and the other not so good. By this time the earth-centered Ptolemaic system had been patched many times to account for the peculiar motions of the planets as revealed by more careful observations over the years. In Copernicus's day, the system was so complicated that he could not believe there wasn't a better solution to the problem of the movement of heavenly bodies.

We know from Copernicus's writings that his ideas grew especially from his knowledge of ideas set forth by two Greek philosophers. One of these, Pythagoras of Samos, was a sixth-century philosopher and mathematician. According to Pythagoras and his followers, the "essence" of the universe was "pure" numbers. The other great influ-

Nicolaus Copernicus

ence was Plato, with his belief that reality resided in ideal forms and that everything material was a kind of shadow world. In a sense, numbers are about as close as one can come to Plato's notion of ideal forms; so mathematics was also an important part of Plato's system of belief. We are told that the entrance to Plato's Academy bore the warning: "Let no one destitute of geometry enter my doors."

These two Greek influences persuaded Copernicus to make his system as simple and mathematical as possible. The simplicity derived largely from modifying Ptolemy's system; Copernicus just exchanged the positions of the sun and the earth. By so doing, he said in the preface to his book describing his system, he was able to reveal the unchangeable symmetry of the parts of the universe concealed by the Ptolemaic system.

That was the good news. The bad news was that Copernicus also firmly believed that all the heavenly motions must be perfect circles. This was near to truth, but not near enough to lead to the correct solution to the problem of movements of heavenly bodies. In any case, the Copernican system was based on a mixture of observations and the conviction derived from Greek thought that only certain ideal motions would be found in the universe, and that what appeared to be other kinds of motions must be due to observational and theoretical error.

The belief that numbers are somehow the essence of things, including the universe, is not the modern view; we don't believe that astronomy is a branch of mathematics, but rather that mathematics is a useful tool for astronomers in pursuing their profession. But this idea in Copernicus's day, which considered numbers as reality rather than a useful tool, once again demonstrates how confusion and misunderstanding serve to promote progress. Many scholars interested in nature, but with no particular interest in mathematics, entered the fold of mathematics because they came to believe, as Copernicus did, that nature was mathematics, and that therefore to know mathematics was to know the universe. No modern scientist believes that studying mathematics for its own sake is the same as probing nature, but no modern physical scientist believes that he could make much progress without mathematics as a tool. Still, modern science believes in its own brand of symmetries as strongly as the Greeks believed in theirs.

As we shall see later, another cherished theory inherited from the Greeks has been abandoned in our time by quantum mechanics, today's theory of the atom and atomic particles. Greek philosophy said that every event must have a well-defined cause, but quantum mechanics, one of the most successful and innovative physical theories of all time, does not agree. The most eminent scientist of our time, Albert Einstein, never did believe that this part of quantum mechanics could be true. But since Einstein's death in 1955, there has been ever-growing evidence that not all natural events in the world can be predicted with certainty even if we know to the last decimal point all of the details leading up to the event. We shall have much more to say about this distinctly non-common sense character of nature in later chapters.

What is common sense one day is not necessarily common sense at a later time. Just as refusal to give up a flat earth for a spherical one left unresolved paradoxes, so refusal to give up the idea of strict cause and effect in quantum mechanics was to leave even worse problems to resolve, as we shall see. But science thrives on paradoxes, and almost always the major advances in science have come with the creation and resolution of a paradox.

As we study the theories that most successfully describe the universe today—from the largest galaxy to the smallest particle—we find that we are a long way from the forces, the pushes and pulls of nature, embedded in the theories of early philosophers and scientists. Sophisticated instruments like radio telescopes and atom smashers help us to look out into space and back in time to the birth of the universe and to examine what goes on inside atoms. Still, although the details of the search have changed, the goals and underlying guides for progress have not. The basic forces and particles of today are only sophisticated versions of their ancestors. Today's quarks and leptons are the great-great-great-grandchildren of the fire, earth, and water that early philosophers supposed made up the world and surrounding heavens. Although quarks and leptons help us understand a good many phenomena that bothered early philosophers—as well as a good many they didn't even know about—the really big discovery was that it was possible to understand the universe in terms of a few components and underlying principles. That the amazing diversity of the universe is something at least partially comprehensible to the human mind is the most profound and amazing discovery of all.

So our tour of the universe will be not only a tour of atoms, molecules, stars, and galaxies, but also a tour of the ideas that have finally led us to believe that the forces that govern the atoms, the stars, and the whole universe, from beginning to possible end, are one. We shall continue our journey now with Isaac Newton, who showed us how to get rid of Atlas and elephants, only to create a space that nobody could find.

3

On the Shoulders of Giants

IN THE DAYS of Copernicus and for a long time afterward, there was no such thing as a scientist in the way we think of scientists today. In fact, the word *scientist* has reached common usage only in this century. Copernicus, reared by an uncle who was a powerful bishop in the Roman Catholic church, was typical of educated men of his day. His understanding of nature was a mixture of alchemy, chemistry, astrology, religious mysticism, and other interests of his time. No clear line separated the study of the motion of the planets and stars as a means of understanding nature from the same study as a means of foretelling the future.

Novel ideas about the universe and man's place in it were as likely to come from a dedicated astrologer as from the clergy or educated noblemen. In the years between 1560 and 1687 several philosophers and observers modified the generally accepted concepts of the universe. We shall look briefly at six of them.

One of the first to embrace wholeheartedly the sun-centered Copernican system was an Italian Dominican monk, Giordano Bruno. Bruno was born five years after Copernicus's book was published, so he knew well the details of the theory, but he went beyond what Copernicus had dared to believe. Bruno said that although the sun was the center of planetary motions, it was in other respects an ordinary star in a universe of infinite extent. He further believed that other stars had their own systems of planets. Although these notions are a cornerstone of modern astronomy, they were heretical in Bruno's time.

Unlike Copernicus, Bruno was an articulate and flamboyant pro-moter of his ideas, and he was also a showman. He comb lectures on his views of the universe with prodigious feats of memory based on a system he had developed himself. Bruno managed to offend practically everyone in authority, and he spent a good deal of his life escaping from one city to the next.

Finally he returned to Rome and was immediately arrested. By then the church had its hands full with the Protestant Reformation movement and was in no mood to move the earth—and presumably God as well—to some obscure corner of the universe. After a seven-year trial, Bruno was sentenced and burned at the stake.

A contemporary of Bruno's, Tycho Brahe, was the son of a Danish nobleman. He was the last, and quite likely the greatest, of the naked-eye astronomers. A firm believer in the earth-centered Ptolemaic system, he was at a loss to reconcile his own observations with that scheme, and if ever a man unintentionally undermined his own position, it was Brahe.

Brahe entered the University of Copenhagen at age thirteen to study law. But a solar eclipse in 1560 captured his imagination, and he turned from law to mathematics and astronomy. As a relatively young man he became famous after discovering a new star that appeared overnight in the heavens. We know now that such stars, *novae* (Latin for new), are not new at all, but are in fact old stars that, under the right conditions, flare into view. But King Frederick II of Denmark was so impressed with Brahe that he became Brahe's patron and allowed him to outfit the finest observatory in Europe.

For the next twenty years, Brahe and his staff doggedly and pains-takingly measured the heavens. They discovered, among other things, that comets do not move in circular orbits—a definite crack in the Greek system of circles. But that was not all. It was clear to Brahe that, in spite of his abiding faith in the Ptolemaic system, something was wrong.

Finally he proposed a system that was something of a compromise between Ptolemy and Copernicus, although it was closer to Ptolemy than to Copernicus. In Brahe's system, the earth sat at the center of the universe, circled by the moon and the sun, but all the other planets and the stars circled the sun. The proposal received wide praise, more for its adherence to Ptolemaic thought than for its scientific merit. Brahe clung to this theory until he died.

In 1600, two weeks before Bruno's execution, Johannes Kepler arrived in Denmark to become guardian of Brahe's treasure of studies and writings. Kepler was a penniless mathematician whom Brahe had

Tycho Brahe's Observatory in Uraniborg, Czechoslovakia

met and greatly admired during a trip to Prague. Before he died that same year, Brahe turned over all of his data to Kepler, imploring him not to let his work have been in vain and to use it to bolster his modified Ptolemaic system.

Kepler distilled Brahe's observations, and in spite of his best intentions, reluctantly concluded that the planets move in near circular, elliptical orbits around the sun. He also spelled out in mathematical detail how the planetary orbital periods were related to their distances from the sun.

After Brahe's comets had put a crack in Greek science with its emphasis on circular motions, the Italian scientist and philosopher Galileo came near to providing the final shattering blow. According to Greek science, the heavier an object was, the faster it fell toward the earth. Legend tells us that Galileo dropped two cannonballs, one ten times heavier than the other, simultaneously from the top of the leaning tower of Pisa, with the result that both balls hit the ground at the same time. Actually Galileo made his discovery by rolling balls of different weight down an inclined plane. He also demonstrated that an object set in motion remains in motion unless some force intervenes to slow it. The Greeks believed that it was necessary to apply a continual force to keep an object in motion.

Although Galileo and Kepler never met, they exchanged letters. Kepler was still very much a part of the alchemy-astrological school of science, and his results concerning the planets, although revolutionary, were often mired in his mystical speculations. In any case, the correspondence did not seem to influence Galileo particularly, because he never mentioned Kepler in any of his books or scientific papers. Kepler on the other hand, famous by this time, was a strong supporter of Galileo's championing of the sun-centered system of the universe.

Galileo had believed from his student days in a sun-centered system; but the telescope, in his hands by 1609, was to provide the final blow to the Ptolemaic system. Curiously enough, the Dutch technicians who had invented the telescope a few years earlier, had not turned it toward the sky. But, after receiving his first primitive telescope, Galileo developed lens-grinding techniques that greatly increased the quality and power of the instrument, and in a period of a few short weeks he revolutionized astronomy.

He learned that the moon had mountains and that the sun was covered with spots. No such blemishes were allowed in Greek science with its perfect circles and spheres. And by following the spots on the sun's surface, he discovered that the sun was not fixed in space but rotated once every twenty-seven days. Another blow to Greek science.

Galileo also directed his telescope toward the planets, with equally amazing results. He saw the moons of Jupiter—more proof that not everything circled the earth—and he saw the phases of Venus in step with its orbit about the sun.

But he was most astounded by his discovery of the rings of Saturn. It is clear from his drawings of Saturn that he saw the rings, but in spite of his own observations, he could not comprehend what he had seen. The sight was so unbelievable that he described the rings as two bodies. He knew he was onto something big, but was so unsure that he presented his results in what is probably the most curious scientific paper of all time; he described his results in an anagram:

smaismrmilmepoetalevmidunenughaviras

After further observations, when he was sure his eyes were not deceiving him, he translated the anagram: "I have observed the highest planet in triplet form."

In 1613 Galileo made public his unqualified endorsement of the Copernican system. Three years later, under threat of imprisonment, he was forced into silence. But then in 1632 a new pope, Urban III,

Galileo

came into power. On the basis of past friendship with the new pope, Galileo decided to resurrect the Copernican system in the form of a dialogue between two experts before an intelligent layman. One expert, Simplicio, represented Ptolemy, and the other represented Copernicus. Galileo imagined that by presenting both sides of the argument, he could avoid angering the church.

Unfortunately, the balanced dialogue was so lopsided in favor of Copernicus that no one was fooled, especially Pope Urban III. In fact, the pope was convinced that Simplicio—the simpleton—represented the church's official position.

And so Galileo, by now old and ill, was forced to retract, in public, his heretical views. The evidence against him was collected by Cardinal Bellarmine, the same cardinal who was instrumental in Bruno's burning at the stake. It is said that Galileo muttered under his breath after his public retraction, "Eppur si muove!" (And yet it moves!), referring to the earth. He spent the rest of his life under house arrest and died in 1642, the year Isaac Newton was born. The Renaissance was on the wane, and with it the open spirit of inquiry.

But Galileo was the last to be imprisoned for supporting the Copernican system because, in spite of the Church's opposition, there was too much momentum behind the methods he had pioneered. No longer could scholars spin theories unsupported by measurement.

Galileo's belief that an object set in motion continued in uniform motion unless some force acted to slow it or accelerate it was a little more restricted than is our belief today. He thought uniform motion was limited to objects traveling in circles, like the earth around the sun or the moon around the earth. Perhaps in this respect he was still under the influence of Greek thought.

In any case, it was the French mathematician and philosopher René Descartes who proposed that objects moving both in circles and in straight lines would continue in their paths forever—in Bruno's infinite universe—if unperturbed. Curiously enough, his belief was based not on experiment but on theology. Or perhaps it's not so curious, considering our review of earlier events.

Descartes believed that the universe, a kind of giant whirlpool, was initially set in motion by God and that it had been running essentially unattended ever since with clocklike, mathematical precision, thus demonstrating the rationality of its maker. The belief that objects continued into the future as they had traveled in the past came naturally from this philosophy. Descartes had considered publishing these ideas in 1633 when he heard of Bruno's execution. Fearing similar treatment at the hands of the Church, he delayed publication for four years.

Descartes's whirlpool, or vortex theory as it is usually called, attempted to explain the motions of the planets set out in Kepler's mathematical portrayal. In terms of Ockham's razor, the theory is an abysmal failure. But it did provide a reason for the planets' moving with coordinated precision around the sun: They were all caught in the giant whirlpool of the universe.

Descartes more than compensated for his cumbersome theorizing, however, by his marriage of algebra and geometry. Kepler had worked out his mathematical descriptions of planetary motion with the tools of Greek geometry—tools hopelessly inadequate for the road Isaac Newton was to take. With Descartes's insight it was possible to provide, through geometry, a spatial interpretation of algebra; and on the other side of the coin, complex geometries could be transformed to algebra for easier manipulation. That is, algebraic symbols could represent geometrical figures and space, while algebraic results could be represented in spatial terms such as a graph. This was just the background Newton needed to develop a whole new branch of mathematics—calculus—in his investigation of gravitation.

Descartes's mathematical invention was tacked on, as an appendix, to his book on vortices in the belief that his "algebraization" of space somehow bolstered his vortex theory. Once again, misunderstanding and confusion were to open a new door. Descartes's wrong-headed, misguided theory contained, in what seemed almost an afterthought, the seeds of an idea that was to flourish under Newton's careful cultivation.

Isaac Newton was born in rather poor circumstances on Christmas Day, 1642, in Woolsthorpe, Lincolnshire, in England. He was reared by his grandparents through his early years and was then sent off to work on his mother's farm. Fortunately, an uncle who was a member of Trinity College at Cambridge recognized that Newton was a poor farmer at best and was potentially a scholar.

With the uncle's blessing, Newton set off for Cambridge in 1660 and graduated with no particular distinction in 1665, the year the Great Plague hit London. During this devastating time, Newton returned to his mother's farm and produced perhaps the greatest intellectual outpouring of all time. In two years he worked out the fundamental features of his theory of gravitation and his laws of motion, practically single-handedly invented the science of optics based on his discoveries using prisms and lenses, and laid the foundations of calculus. And all this by the age of twenty-four.

The optical work made Newton famous, and he returned to Cambridge in 1667, where he remained for thirty years. But his work on motion, gravitation, and calculus remained almost unknown for nearly twenty years. Then in 1684 the English scientist Robert Hooke boasted to the famous architect Sir Christopher Wren and astronomer Edmund Halley—after whom Halley's Comet is named—that he had worked out the laws governing the planetary motions. Wren was not impressed with Hooke's explanation, and he offered a reward to anyone who could present a satisfactory explanation of planetary motions.

In the meantime, Halley went to see his friend Newton and asked him if he had any explanation. Newton immediately replied that he had worked out the problem some years earlier and was able to show mathematically why the planets move in elliptical orbits, as Kepler had discovered, under the influence of gravity.

In a state of great excitement, Halley asked Newton to let him see his calculations. Newton discovered that he had misplaced them in the intervening years and so had to redo them, which he did in a very brief time.

Halley was astounded; and being a man of some wealth, he personally financed Newton's book *Mathematical Principles of Natural Philosophy*, perhaps the greatest scientific treatise of all time. While the greatest minds of the last half of the seventeenth century were trying to discover the secret of gravitation, Newton had already found it and lost it, then explained it again. But as Newton said of himself, "If I have seen further than other men, it is because I stood on the shoulders of giants." Certainly two of those giants were Kepler and Galileo, and Descartes had provided the seed for Newton's invention of calculus.

Like all other great theories in science, Newton's work was a bringing together of past work to create a new whole whose power vastly exceeded the power of its parts. The Greeks had thought earthly and cosmic motions were governed by different sets of laws. Newton showed them to be one and the same.

Newton's grand plan for the universe was a scheme not even Ockham could have dreamed of. All the heavenly and earthly motions—from infinite past into infinite future—were condensed into a set of laws that can be written in less than half a page. The French philosopher and wit Voltaire was captivated by Newton's methods. Commenting

Sir Isaac Newton

on a Norwegian expedition to the North Pole—to see if the earth
was slightly flat at the poles as one might expect, for a spinning planet
would bulge at the equator and flatten at the poles—he said that
"these poor fools had set out, at the risk of life and limb, to prove
what Newton had discovered in his library."

The general public was also caught up in the enthusiasm. Many
popular books appeared. One of the most readable was titled *Sir
Isaac Newton's Philosophy for the Use of Ladies*. But still, as Newton
himself admitted, there were problems. Descartes's whirlpool theory,
although wrong, had provided a plausible reason for the planets' move-

ment around the sun; in Newton's theory the equations gave unheard-of accuracy but provided not the slightest material clue as to why they worked. This point was not missed by Newton, and as we shall see later, it required a restructuring of the universe by Albert Einstein, perhaps not to resolve the problem, but at least to cast it in a new way.

But first we shall have a closer look at Newton's grand plan, at his law of gravitation and his three laws of motion. It was a plan sufficiently powerful to land man on the moon, but philosophically so unsatisfactory that, like Copernicus's theory, it was considered at first to be little more than a computational device. This view prevailed in most of Europe for over a hundred years after Newton's death.

4

Where's the Ether?

NEWTON'S CONCEPT of the universe portrays all events played out on a vast, infinite stage called space and time. Time in Newton's scheme is the same for everyone, no matter what his location or motion. Newton's space is the three-dimensional space of elementary geometry books—the kind of space first studied by Euclid. All objects in this space move according to three laws of motion.

The first of Newton's three laws is a distillation and expansion of Descartes's and Galileo's idea that objects once set in motion continue forever unless some force intercedes to change their motion—the force of friction that slows a brick sliding over a frozen lake, perhaps, or a brief rocket burst to fine-tune the path of a spaceship drifting toward a distant planet.

The early Greek philosophers thought just the opposite: the natural state of an object they thought to be at rest, and they believed an object moves only so long as some force acts on it. But if this were so, man-launched earth satellites would begin their fall toward earth at the end of the last rocket blast boosting them into orbit.

Newton's first law is generally referred to as the law of *inertia* because inertia is the quality of an object that embodies its reluctance to move if it is at rest, or to change its constant, straight-line motion if it is moving.

The general principle seems simple enough, but it is full of booby traps. In a tug-of-war, the opposing contestants split into two teams on either side of a line drawn on the ground. The team members on both sides grasp a long length of rope and try to pull each other's team over the line. During the struggle both teams are obviously

Fig. 1. As long as the net force is zero, there is no movement.

pulling, but there may or may not be movement of the rope. If both sides pull with equal force, in opposite directions, there will be no movement. In other words, the net force on the rope is zero.

Newton's first law reflects this observation because it says, in part, that a body at rest remains at rest as long as the net force acting on it is zero. But if one team begins to pull harder than the other, we will see a change from no motion to motion in the direction of the team pulling with the greater force.

Let's suppose now that our tug-of-war takes place not on the earth's surface, but on the bed of a long railroad flatcar moving with constant speed along a straight section of track. The line scratched on the ground is replaced by a chalk line across the middle of the flatcar. Let's suppose that we are standing on the flatcar watching the teams pulling with equal force in opposite directions, so that the rope does not move with respect to the chalk line. From our point of view, we would say that the net force on the rope is zero and therefore the rope does not move (fig. 1).

But what of an observer on the ground watching the train going by? He would see the contestants move past him along with the train.

Does this mean that the contestants at the front of the flatcar are winning because those at the rear are moving in the same direction as the contestants at the front are pulling? Obviously not. What counts is the motion of the contestants relative to the chalk mark, not their motion relative to the ground.

In other words, the net force on an object is the same whether the object is viewed by someone at rest with respect to the object or by someone who is moving with constant speed and direction relative to the object. More simply, we can say that Newton's first law is the same for bodies in a state of rest or in uniform motion.

If we put all of these considerations together, we come up with Newton's first law: Every object stays in a state of rest or in uniform straight-line motion unless an unbalanced force acts on it.

How do we know when a body is at rest or is in constant, straight-line motion? If two spaceships pass in deep interstellar space where no planets or stars are in view, how do we decide their motion? Could we say that one spaceship was at rest while the other passed by? Or could we say with equal validity that both moved in their encounter? As we have seen, Newton's first law is valid in either case; all we require is uniform relative motion—*inertial frames of reference*, as Newton called them. That's a term we must remember.

And how do we know if a frame of reference is an inertial frame? That's easy. It's a frame where Newton's first law is true. Not so fast, you may say. Aren't we arguing in circles?

If you've ever sat in a train beside another train in a railroad station, you have doubtless experienced the problem of "who is moving and who isn't." Often you have the sense of motion but you aren't sure whether it's your train or the one on a nearby track that is moving. It's only when you look beyond the neighboring train to some fixed object—the corner of the station perhaps—that you can resolve the problem. That is, you establish what we commonly understand to be motion, or lack of motion, with respect to some other object that is anchored firmly to the earth.

In our everyday life we almost always measure motion with respect to the earth. We say an object is moving if it changes its position relative to the earth's surface, and that it is at rest if it does not. But we know that the earth circles the sun, and that the sun moves relative to the stars making up our galaxy, and that our galaxy moves relative to the galaxies in its neighborhood, and so on. So where does that leave us or take us, literally? By the corner of what "train station" in

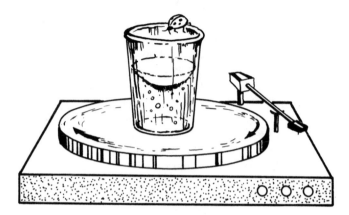

Fig. 2. Newton believed that the concave surface of the water proved that absolute space exists.

the universe are we to measure the motions of baseballs, trains, planets, stars, galaxies, and whole systems of galaxies?

If you find the question troublesome, you're in good company because the question greatly bothered Newton. In his book *Mathematical Principles of Natural Philosophy*, he wrote, "For it may be that there is no body, really at rest, to which the places and motions of others may be referred." Newton finally decided that empty space itself defined an absolute reference system against which the motion of all objects could be judged. But what does this mean? How do we drive a spike in empty space against which to measure the motion of an object?

Newton thought the existence of absolute space could be proved not by objects moving in straight lines, but by spinning objects. Imagine placing a glass of water in the center of a record-player turntable. As the turntable begins to spin, the water, because of its inertia, does not immediately spin with the same rotation as the glass, but gradually picks up speed until finally it rotates in step with the glass.

If you were a small bug sitting on the edge of the glass, it would appear to you that the water was completely still with respect to the glass. But you would notice one peculiar thing—a pronounced dip in the level of the water at the center of the glass. Even though the water is not moving with respect to the glass, it "knows," according to Newton, that it is rotating with respect to absolute space. The curved surface of the water, Newton said, is proof that absolute space exists. But other observers, including in particular one of Newton's contemporaries, have not been entirely happy with Newton's spinning glass of water as proof of absolute space, (fig. 2).

Newton's first law is assumed to be a universal law. That is, it is believed to apply at any place or at any time in the universe, and to all objects, be they popcorn balls, hockey pucks, or electrons. This may seem to be obvious today, but at the time it was a bold step and another example of Ockham's dictum to explain the most with the least.

The first law says that the states of rest and of uniform motion are equivalent because both represent the case where the net force acting on a body is zero. What happens to an object when the net force is *not* zero? This is the subject of Newton's second law.

Let's imagine that we are pulling a sled over a frozen lake so that we can ignore, for all practical purposes, the friction between the sled runners and the ice. Instead of pulling directly on the sled, though, we hook a spring scale to the front of the sled and a handle to the other end of the scale so that by pulling on the handle we indirectly pull on the sled (fig. 3). As we begin to pull on the handle, the sled picks up speed, or accelerates, and we notice that the scale registers a certain value—say 5 pounds.

As long as we pull the sled so that the scale always registers 5 pounds, the sled continues to accelerate at a steady rate, but if we pull harder, so that the scale registers 10 pounds, then the sled acceler-

Fig. 3. Acceleration depends on force and mass.

ates at an even faster rate and continues at this rate as long as we pull, so that the scale always shows 10 pounds. In other words, the rate at which the sled accelerates increases as we pull harder.

If we did enough experiments with our sled, we'd find that doubling the pulling force—from 5 to 10 pounds, for example—doubles the rate of acceleration; if we triple the pulling force, the acceleration triples, and so on. In other words, the acceleration is directly proportional to the net force acting on a body. This is the first fact we need to know to formulate Newton's second law.

The other fact has to do with the inertia or *mass* of the object acted upon by the force. The mass of an object is a measure of its inertia. Let's do some more experiments now in which we pull the sled in such a way that the scale always registers 5 pounds. But this time we'll use sleds made from different materials—aluminum, iron, lead, and so forth. What we will notice is that if our pulling force is always kept at 5 pounds, the sled made from aluminum will accelerate faster than the one made from iron, and the one made from iron faster than the one made from lead. In other words, for a given force the acceleration decreases directly in proportion to the mass, or inertia, of the object on which the force acts. This is the second fact we need.

Now let's put our two facts together. The acceleration of an object is directly proportional to the force acting on it, but decreases in direct proportion to the mass of the object. If we let a stand for acceleration, m for mass, and f for the force acting on an object, then we can state the second law in very compact form:

$$a = f/m$$

or what amounts to the same thing,

$$f = ma$$

which is the more customary way to express Newton's second law. We should add, for completeness, that the direction in which the object accelerates is the same direction in which the force acts.

This law, like the first law, is thought to be universal. It makes no difference whether the force is mechanical, electrical, gravitational, or whatever; and again, the object can be of any material whatever; and finally, the law applies at any time, any place in the universe.

Fig. 4. For every action there is an equal and opposite reaction.

Let's summarize what we know: the first law tells us what happens to an object when there is no net force acting on it, and the second law tells us what happens when there is a net force. Newton defined a force as any action that causes an object to accelerate. This force must be external to the object; an object can't alter its own motion, any more than a person can lift himself by pulling on his bootstraps.

But if the force is external, what can we say about the outside object responsible for the force? To complete the picture we need to say something about how the agent producing the external force is connected to or altered by the object being acted upon. Here the Greek idea of symmetry comes to our aid. We might suspect that in some sense what happens to the object being acted upon happens in reverse to the agent doing the acting. For example, if we push on a large rock, we are the external agent and we feel the rock resisting, as though it is pushing back against us (fig. 4).

Newton summarized this symmetry between the agent and the object acted upon in his third law of motion: For every action there is an equal and opposite reaction.

We have said that an object can't alter its own motion. What about an athlete running the one-hundred-meter dash? Isn't he altering his own motion without any external agent? No, because his shoes are in contact with the earth, and the earth "pushes back" with a force that matches the force of his feet against the earth.

Any time a body changes its motion—speeds up, slows down, changes direction, or all three—the change is caused by a force that is paired with some reacting force. Sometimes the reaction is not obvious, especially when one of the objects is much more massive than the other. But the running athlete alters the motion of the earth—ever so slightly—as he races along the track. It really doesn't make any difference which we call the action and which the reaction, because they happen at the same time. When things happen at the same time, we can't say that one caused the other. This notion in Newton's third law, that action and reaction occur at the same time, will turn out to be a problem, as we shall see later.

As with Newton's first and second laws, the third law is thought to be universal, independent of the kind of forces involved or the nature of the objects. And as with the other laws, it holds for any time or place in the universe.

Now let's consider Newton's three laws in connection with a particular kind of force, the *gravitational* force, as we call it today. As we shall see in Chapter 9, this is a very peculiar force indeed, and it is this peculiarity as much as anything else that led Einstein to reformulate Newton's law of gravity into a new theory of gravity—the General Theory of Relativity. But we must save those details until we have a closer look at Newton's theory of gravity.

Let's assume that we know Newton's three laws of motion along with Kepler's deduction that the planets move in elliptical orbits around the sun, and we set for ourselves the following problem: What is the nature of the force that would explain the elliptical motions of the planets? This is the problem that faced Newton when he set out to solve the mystery of planetary motion.

We don't know just what went through Newton's mind, but it may have been something like this: From the first law of motion, the planets should move in straight lines unless some force causes them to move in curved paths. Since all the planets move in curved paths around the sun, it seems likely that there is a force associated with the sun acting along a line connecting the sun to the planets. Furthermore, if the sun can exert a force on the planets, then it seems reasonable that the planets exert a force on the sun. Here is another example of the Greek belief in symmetry, and also an application of the third law of motion. Finally, the force is probably a universal force, and so it should apply to apples falling to the ground as well as to planets circling the sun.

As we know from Chapter 3, Galileo had discovered that all bodies, independent of weight, fall toward the earth with the same acceleration. This means that the gravitational force must somehow increase in direct proportion to the mass of the object it is acting on.

At this point we need to digress a bit to say something about the difference between mass and weight. In our everyday language we tend to use the two words interchangeably, but strictly speaking this is not correct. The *weight* of an object depends on the strength of the gravitational field it is in. An object like a large rock that weighs 6 pounds on the earth, weighs about 1 pound on the moon because the force of gravity on the moon is about a sixth as great as it is on the earth.

The *mass* of the rock, however, is the same in both places because mass, according to Newton's first law, is related to the resistance an object shows to changing its state of motion, whether it is at rest or in constant straight-line motion. In other words, it would be much easier to pick up the rock on the moon than on the earth because it weighs less on the moon, but if we were to tie a length of cord to the rock and swing it in a circle about our head, it would take just as much effort on the moon as on the earth because the *mass* of the cord and the rock are the same in both places.

The nice thing about mass is that it is defined in such a way that its value is independent of gravitational force; and so Newton's laws of motion, written in terms of mass, apply unambiguously anywhere in·the universe. If his laws were written in terms of the weight of an object, we would have to specify where in the universe we were making our measurements because the force of gravitation would make the weight different at different places.

Mass is one of those quantities that physicists are always seeking because they don't change value in different situations. Physicists say that mass is an invariant quantity because it always maintains its value no matter how we look at it, whereas weight is not an invariant quantity. A good deal of physics is concerned with searching out invariant quantities because they represent a kind of underlying structure to the universe that is not subject to alteration. We should add that Einstein generalized the idea of mass to include energy as well; we shall say more about this later.

It seems likely that if bodies with mass are the source of gravitational forces, those forces should decrease with distance from the mass producing them—in the same sense that the light from a candle grows dimmer as we move away from the candle. And finally, it seems reasonable that the more massive the body, the greater the gravitational force associated with it.

If we put all of these thoughts about gravity together, we come up with the idea that the gravitational force between two bodies is something like this: The force acts along a line connecting the two bodies, increases as the masses of the bodies increase, and decreases as the distance between them increases. This is a good start, but to have a law we need to be specific as to *how* a gravitational force depends on mass and distance.

Newton may have tinkered around with a number of possibilities, but he finally hit on a simple version that yielded, in detail, the elliptical orbits of the planets around the sun. First, he said, the force decreases with the square of the distance between the two bodies. This simply means that every time we double the distance, the force decreases by a factor of four—not two, which is a plausible guess but one that won't account for the planetary motions.

Second, the force increases in direct proportion to the masses of the two bodies multiplied by each other. So, for example, if the mass of either of the bodies increases by a factor of two, the force doubles, and so on.

To complete the story we need to consider a huge problem that faced Newton at this point: How was he to calculate the gravitational force between two bodies such as the sun and the earth? The problem is that every little bit of matter anywhere in the earth has a mutual attraction with every other little bit of matter anywhere in the sun. To add up all these elementary forces acting over different distances to obtain the total force would be a never-ending job, so Newton created a new branch of mathematics, calculus, to do the job. With calculus he showed that the entire mass of the sun could be considered to reside at the center of the sun, and similarly, the mass of the earth could be considered to reside at the center of the earth; so the only distance that need be considered is the distance from the center of the sun to the center of the earth. This transformed an endless task into one simple calculation.

No theory before Newton's work even came close to his laws of motion and gravitation in terms of simplicity, elegance, and scope of application. A handful of equations explained the motions of the planets and the moon, the bulge at the earth's equator, the ocean tides, the trajectory of a cannonball, and the variation in the period of a pendulum with latitude. For Newton's laws of motion, unlike earlier formulas, applied to mass whatever its form, be it a cannonball, the oceans, or the sun. The great English poet Alexander Pope wrote:

> *Nature and Nature's laws lay hid in night:*
> *God said, Let Newton be! and all was light.*

But not *all* was light. No one denied that Newton's equations had unheard-of power, but what was this strange force connecting planets to each other and to the sun—connections over millions and hundreds of millions of miles? How could one body exert a force on another with no visible connection? It was as though a horse could pull a wagon merely by walking in front of it. There was a strong feeling, especially in Europe, that Newton's explanation, although marvelously useful, was little more than an efficient computational scheme—a charge directed earlier toward Copernicus's sun-centered solar system.

It seemed to many that there must be some substance filling Newton's infinite stage of space and time—*ether* it was called. With ether it was possible to imagine that the gravitational force somehow rippled through the universe in much the same way that dropping a stone in a lake sends out a system of waves that can cause a distant cork to bob up and down as the wave passes by.

Newton too was bothered. He wrote, "It is inconceivable that inanimate brute matter should, without the mediation of something else . . . affect other matter without mutual contact. . . ."

Some suggested that the ether should be identified with the absolute frame of reference Newton thought he had demonstrated with his "glass" of rotating water. That is, the water "knew" it was rotating with respect to some absolute frame of space; otherwise, why would it slide up the side of the glass?

Others felt that since there was not the slightest evidence that ether existed, some other explanation of the curved water surface should be sought. One of the most vocal opponents of the idea of absolute space—and therefore of ether—was an Irish philosopher, economist, mathematician, and bishop, George Berkeley. He argued that all motion is relative, and there is no such thing as absolute space—and therefore no ether. So we are at liberty to pick any frame as an inertial frame of reference and measure all others against it. Berkeley further stated that one cannot talk about motion of only one object in space. That is, motion with respect to space doesn't mean anything; how could one know if he had moved from one part of space to another? Motion, Berkeley argued, means something only if there are other objects in space with respect to which one can move.

Berkeley finally concluded that it was the distribution of fixed stars throughout the universe that provide the reference points by which the motion of objects could be judged. The rotating glass "knows" that it is rotating relative to the distant stars, he argued. The frame-of-reference problem has not been solved completely to this day, although the General Theory of Relativity, which we shall discuss in Chapter 9, adds new insights.

Like Professor Bohr's horseshoe, Newton's theories worked even if one didn't believe in them—ether or no ether, absolute space or no absolute space. All that counts is frames of reference moving in constant, straight-line motion. The game of billiards works just as well on a smoothly cruising ship crossing the sea as it does on land.

In spite of Bishop Berkeley's doubts, it was hard to believe there was not some ether-filled frame of reference against which all other motion could be measured in some absolute sense. Yet there was not one scrap of evidence that ether existed. In any case, Berkeley and others who followed him started a chant that continued until the present century: "Where's the ether?" Next we shall follow the development of a new theory of electricity and magnetism that pointed the way to the end of the search for the elusive ether.

5

Rediscovering the Atom

IN 1958 NIELS BOHR attended a lecture by a prominant physicist who described a new theory he believed represented an important contribution to science. After much discussion the whimsical Bohr rose and said, "We are all agreed that your theory is crazy. The question which divides us is whether it is crazy enough."

Newton's gravitational theory had been just crazy enough to predict, with great accuracy, the interactions of celestial bodies and at the same time explain the behavior of waterfalls and leaves dropping to earth. But Newton had known there was more to the story than gravitational force. He wrote, "There are therefore agents in nature able to make particles of bodies stick together by very strong attractions. And it is the business of experimental philosophy to find them out."

Newton knew that whatever these forces were, they were far stronger than the force of gravity. If we place two locomotives a few feet apart on a railroad track, they do not inch toward each other under mutual gravitational attraction. It is only with massive bodies like the sun and the earth that gravitation becomes visible. So whatever it is that holds a steel bar, a bowling ball, or a diamond together, it is not the force of gravity. Here we need some new explanation, possibly crazier than the one Newton concocted for gravitation.

One of the most obvious non-gravitational forces known in Newton's age and much earlier was the strange force that caused a compass needle to align itself in a north-south direction. Here is another instance of some invisible force reaching out and interacting with matter, but this force greatly exceeds the gravitational force: Two locomotive-size magnets within a few feet of each other would immediately crash

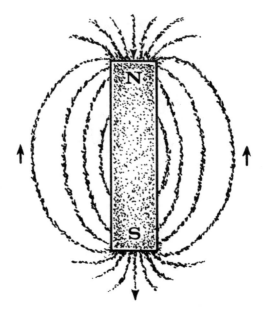

Fig. 1. The iron filings reveal the magnetic lines of force.

together just as two small bar magnets jump together on a lesser scale.

With these much stronger forces at work, why hasn't the universe crashed in on itself, or possibly exploded outward? The answer is that magnetic force, unlike gravitational force, comes in two varieties—an attractive force and a repulsive force. Under the gravitational force, objects are always attracted to each other, whereas with magnetic force there may be attraction or repulsion. We know that pressing the "north" or positive poles of two bar magnets together generates a repulsive force, whereas a positive and a negative pole attract each other.

Perhaps in a science class you have experimented with magnets and iron filings. If so, you know how iron filings sprinkled on a paper lying directly over a bar magnet arrange themselves in spidery trails that connect the positive and negative poles of the magnet. These trails show that the lines of magnetic force do not spread out into space like the gravitational force, but connect with the two ends of the magnet (fig. 1).

Why not just slice off two or three thin slices of, say, the positive pole and make magnets with just positive poles? We might expect such a "positive pole only" magnet under a sheet of paper covered with iron filings to show lines of force radiating outward into space. But what we find is that the slice we cut off now has both a positive and a negative pole. Nature seems to insist that the positive and negative poles must balance; every time we create one pole, we also create the other.

So unlike the gravitational force, magnetic forces always balance because of equal numbers of positive and negative poles, and this is why magnetic forces do not cause the universe to collapse or explode. Added up, throughout space, the net force is zero, and we know from Newton's first law that a change in motion requires a net force other than zero. In terms of our tug-of-war analogy, we can think of magnetic forces as consisting of an almost infinite number of miniature tug-of-war battles with nobody winning.

Gravity and magnetism were not the only forces known in Newton's time. It was not uncommon to hear stories of people's hair standing on end during a violent thunderstorm, and of course the power of lightning to shatter trees and to kill or injure animals and people was well known.

Electric force, like magnetic force, is both attractive and repulsive. That is, there is positive electricity and negative electricity; objects with like charges—all positive or all negative—repel each other, and bodies with opposite charges attract each other. And as with magnetic forces, there seems to be as much negative electricity in the universe as positive; so on the average, the electric forces cancel out and leave no net force to act on the universe as a whole. Compared to gravity, the electric force is very strong. If a battleship should accumulate a net imbalance of just one percent in electrical charge, the energy would be enough to launch the battleship out of the solar system.

At first no one thought there was any connection between electricity and magnetism. But then in 1820 the Danish scientist Hans Christian Øersted discovered by chance that the magnetized needle of a compass changed direction in the vicinity of a wire carrying an electric current. The electric current apparently "looked like" another magnet to the magnetized needle. And then later, in 1831, an English experimenter, Michael Faraday, discovered that a changing magnetic force produces an electric current. For example, if we move a bar magnet in and out of a coil of wire, current will flow in the wire. It appears to the

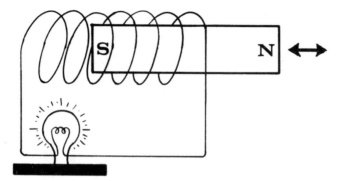

Fig. 2. A changing magnetic field produces an electric current.

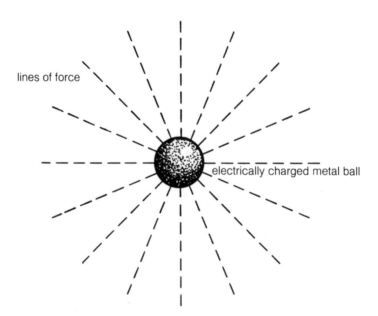

Fig. 3. The electric force lessens with distance from the electric charge.

wire that the magnetic force is changing because the magnet is alternately close to the wire and away from the wire (fig. 2). Today we use that fact to produce electricity at electrical power plants.

Øersted's and Faraday's discoveries were clear evidence that electricity and magnetism are intimately related because either one, under the right circumstances, seemed to be able to produce the other. Once more we see symmetry at work in nature.

Faraday tried to explain his observations as well as Øersted's in terms of what he called *field lines* of force. Probably his interpretation was greatly influenced by the patterns produced by iron filings. Faraday imagined that the forces responsible for the interactions between two magnets, two electric currents, or a magnet and an electric current were produced by invisible lines of force, and that the density of the field lines—electric or magnetic—at any point in space was a measure of the strength of the force at that point (Fig. 3). As one moved farther and farther away from the source of a force, an electrically charged metal ball perhaps, this force weakened because the field lines grew less and less dense as they spread out through space. The field lines were probably supported by some etherlike substance— perhaps the same ether many thought essential to explain the gravitational force that operated throughout the universe.

Faraday believed firmly in the unity of nature. He believed that somehow everything is connected—a belief that was well-founded with respect to electricity and magnetism—but he also suspected that light was somehow connected with electricity and magnetism. We know something of his ideas because of an unplanned talk he gave in 1846. Faraday was to introduce a well-known English physicist, Sir Charles Wheatstone, to an audience at the Royal Institution of London. At the last moment, Wheatstone bolted into the street with stage fright, so Faraday, not knowing what to do, gave an extemporaneous talk himself.

Normally he would have confined his remarks to things he had verified experimentally, but this time he allowed himself the luxury of some speculation. He suggested that light might be vibrating lines of electric or magnetic force. He did not have the mathematical skills to develop his idea, however, and those in the audience probably did not understand his concept of lines of force well enough to pursue the matter. But ten years later, a young mathematical physicist, James Clerk Maxwell, who had just graduated from Cambridge University, had enough skill and understanding to bring the matter to a brilliant conclusion.

**Faraday's laboratory
at the Royal Institution**

The first hint that Maxwell was looking into Faraday's lines of
force came in 1854 with publication of a paper aptly titled, "On Faraday's Lines of Force." It was clear from this work that Maxwell brought
a good deal of mathematical skill to the subject. Seven years later,
in 1861, he confided to Faraday that light was indeed a form of electrical-
magnetic vibration, as Faraday had suspected. Maxwell revealed the
full details in 1864, in a scientific paper titled "A Dynamical Theory
of the Electro-magnetic Field," which did for electricity and magnetism
what Newton's work had done for motion and gravity.

Maxwell had taken the known facts about electricity and magnetism and formed them into four compact equations. Two of the facts

related how the fields of magnetic poles and electric charges spread throughout space. A third fact was Faraday's discovery that changing magnetic fields produce electric currents, and the fourth was Øersted's discovery that electric currents produce magnetic fields.

This fourth idea seemed incomplete to Maxwell. If changing magnetic fields could produce electric currents, why couldn't changing electric fields produce magnetic fields? So great was Maxwell's faith in the symmetry of nature that he boldly amended his equations to reflect that idea. It was a brilliant stroke because it was just what was needed to predict the existence of electromagnetic waves. With his four equations, Maxwell was able to show that changing electric and magnetic fields could regenerate each other, over and over, producing a wave that travels on forever through space. Furthermore, the equations predicted the speed of this new wave: it was exactly the measured speed of light. As Maxwell said in his paper: "The agreement of the results seems to show that . . . light is an electromagnetic disturbance propagated through the field according to electromagnetic laws."

Maxwell died at age forty-eight, nine years before the German physicist Heinrich Hertz confirmed Maxwell's prediction in detail. Today we know that all kinds of waves, including infrared waves and visible light waves, are forms of electromagnetic radiation. With Maxwell's four equations we understand the wave nature of everything from X rays to radio waves, and the electric and magnetic forces were forged into a single new force, the electromagnetic force. In Newton's time it appeared that there were three basic forces in nature—gravitational, electrical, and magnetic. But with Maxwell's theory most scientists believed by 1888 that all the universe was ruled by two forces—the gravitational and the electromagnetic.

It remained to be seen whether ether was really essential for propagating gravitational and electromagnetic forces. Perhaps the ether was just a "scaffold" erected by Newton and Maxwell during formulation of their theories, which could be removed once the theories were complete. And then again maybe the scaffold was an essential element of the theories. Nobody knew. In any case, Maxwell seemed convinced of the necessity of ether, for he wrote: "Whatever difficulties we may have in forming a consistent idea of the constitution of ether, there can be no doubt that interplanetary space and interstellar space are not empty, but are occupied by a material substance or body, which is certainly the largest, and probably the most uniform body of which we have any knowledge. . . ."

But as we shall see, Einstein showed near the turn of the century that Maxwell had unknowingly constructed his theory in just such a way that it cast extreme doubt on the existence of ether. Like Tycho Brahe, who undermined his own belief in the Ptolemaic system through his careful observations, Maxwell had provided one of the key pieces of evidence casting doubt on the existence of the very substance he believed necessary to sustain electromagnetic waves.

We have discussed the forces that interact with objects, but have said very little about these objects themselves, except to mention that they have a universal property called mass. Some of the early

Greek philosophers, especially Democritus, believed that all matter consists of tiny particles so small that nothing could be smaller. He called these particles *atoms*, which in Greek means "indivisible." He imagined that the atoms were something like identical, interchangeable building blocks, with different kinds of atoms for different kinds of substances. The "water" atoms were smooth and round and easily slid by each other, whereas the "earth" atoms were rough and jagged so that they stuck together to form durable, hard substances. Substances that have different forms—like liquid, solid, and vapor in the case of water, for example—merely represented different patterns of the same basic atom. Democritus further believed that the spaces between atoms were simply empty space—a vacuum.

Democritus's ideas are not too far from our modern concept of the atom, but his views were overshadowed by Socrates's views of the universe. Socrates believed that all matter could be divided into pieces as small as one liked. That is, there were no atoms. He further believed that there was no such thing as empty space. "Nature abhors a vacuum," he said. We see here, even in ancient times, the belief that all space is filled with some etherlike substance.

The views of Democritus and Socrates represent two views of nature that have been in and out of favor ever since they were first proposed. In one view matter is particle-like—discrete and indestructible. In the other view, matter is simply a concentration here and there of the basic, indivisible "stuff"—perhaps the ether?—of the universe, much as a wave or whirlpool in a river is a local rearrangement of the underlying material, water. As we shall see in Chapter 6, the modern view is that matter is *both* particle-like and wavelike.

Before the middle of the eighteenth century, chemistry was much like physics and astronomy had been during Copernicus's life. It was a mixture of about half superstition and half fact. But the invention of a new kind of very accurate scale, the analytic balance, did for chemistry what the telescope had done for astronomy. With the analytic balance, chemists could measure very accurately just what proportions of various substances were needed to produce new substances.

In some cases the mixture didn't make any difference. If we mix salt with pepper, for example, we can mix in as much of each as we like because we are not forming anything new; we have simply intermingled particles of pepper and salt, as we can easily verify with a magnifying glass.

But mixing chlorine gas with the puttylike metal sodium is a different matter. Here if we mix in too much of one or the other, we have some chlorine or sodium left over, depending on which one we added in excess. Furthermore, the chlorine and sodium disappear and form a new substance with properties entirely different from either sodium or chlorine. If we taste this new substance we know at once what it is—salt.

With the analytic balance a chemist could tell that to make salt he needed exactly 35 parts of chlorine to 23 parts of sodium by weight. With any different proportions there was always some sodium or chlorine left over. It seemed clear to the English chemist John Dalton that this exacting proportion was easy to understand if one assumed that there were sodium atoms and chlorine atoms. Imagine, he suggested, that each sodium atom joins with a chlorine atom to form what he called a *molecule* of salt. If there were not exactly the same number of sodium and chlorine atoms, one or the other would be left over at the end of the chemical reaction forming salt.

And why does the reaction require exactly 35 parts of chlorine to 23 parts of sodium? That's easy too, said Dalton. The chlorine atom simply weighs 35/23 as much as the sodium atom. By 1810 most of the chemists of the world were persuaded by Dalton's argument, and it appeared that Democritus was right and Socrates was wrong. The atom had been rediscovered.

Further investigation, using the analytic balance to measure the proportions needed to make molecules from different kinds of atoms, showed that hydrogen was the lightest of all the atoms. Scientists agreed to say arbitrarily that the mass—atomic mass as it is called—of the hydrogen atom would be 1, with all other masses given relative to the mass of the hydrogen atom. In this scheme the oxygen atom has a mass of 16 because it has 16 times as much mass as the hydrogen atom; chlorine has a mass of 35.5, and so on. In later years the atomic masses were redefined in terms of the oxygen atom because it combined with so many different kinds of atoms, but the principle remained the same.

Today we call a substance that consists of only one kind of atom—gold, aluminum, oxygen, or whatever—an *element,* and substances made by joining different kinds of atoms we call *compounds.* Water is a compound of two hydrogen atoms and one oxygen atom—H_2O.

After the world was convinced of Dalton's atomic theory, it returned with renewed interest to Newton's question: What is the strong force that holds objects together? But perhaps there wasn't a force.

Maybe atoms had hooks that joined with hooks on other atoms to form tightly bound substances. In any case, it looked as though atoms were not the simple, indivisible hard objects that Democritus had imagined. It was time to investigate the atom.

But how does one investigate something as small as the atom was supposed to be? Using normal, laboratory-size tools would be like trying to take a watch apart with a grappling hook—a watch that the investigator couldn't even see.

Fortunately, there was a good deal to be learned about the atom without taking it apart. In the years following Dalton's work, much was discovered about the ways in which the basic elements react with each other to form new compounds. One of the most curious patterns had to do with the number of atoms with which the atom of a particular element would combine to form a molecule. Sodium, for example, would combine with only one other atom, whereas oxygen would combine with either one or two other atoms; oxygen combines with two hydrogen atoms to form water, for example.

This combining power of atoms was called *valence*, which in Latin means "power". Atoms that combine with only one other atom have a valence of one; those that can combine with two other atoms, a valence of two, and so on. The scientists who suspected that atoms had hooks thought that one-valence atoms had one hook, two-valence atoms had two hooks, and so on.

A Russian chemist, Dmitry Ivanovich Mendeleyev, was convinced that there must be some underlying pattern connected with the mass and valence of atoms. To help with his search, he took a stack of blank cards and marked each card with one of the basic elements along with its atomic mass. One card he labeled hydrogen and marked it with its mass number 1; another, labeled carbon, he marked with its mass number 12, and so on through all sixty-three of the elements known at that time.

After much rearranging of his cards, Mendeleyev discovered a particular grid arrangement that sorted the cards by both atomic mass and valence number. In this arrangement he realized that chemicals with similar physical and chemical properties lined up in columns with the same valence number (see table).

To appreciate Mendeleyev's delight and astonishment, let's consider a similar situation. Suppose you are not familiar with playing cards and someone hands you a shuffled deck with a few cards missing. You are asked to see if you can find any pattern running through the

PERIODIC CLASSIFICATION OF THE ELEMENTS

The atomic number is given above the symbol of the element; the atomic weight, below the symbol. Values in parentheses are mass numbers of radioactive elements.

PERIODS	Group 1	2										3	4	5	6	7	8	0
1	1 H 1.00797																	2 He 4.0026
2	3 Li 6.939	4 Be 9.0122										5 B 10.811	6 C 12.01115	7 N 14.0067	8 O 15.9994	9 F 18.9984	10 Ne 20.183
3	11 Na 22.9898	12 Mg 24.312										13 Al 26.9815	14 Si 28.086	15 P 30.9738	16 S 32.064	17 Cl 35.453	18 Ar 39.948
4	19 K 39.102	20 Ca 40.08	21 Sc 44.956	22 Ti 47.90	23 V 50.942	24 Cr 51.996	25 Mn 54.9380	26 Fe 55.847	27 Co 58.9332	28 Ni 58.71	29 Cu 63.54	30 Zn 65.37	31 Ga 69.72	32 Ge 72.59	33 As 74.9216	34 Se 78.96	35 Br 79.909	36 Kr 83.80
5	37 Rb 85.47	38 Sr 87.62	39 Y 88.905	40 Zr 91.22	41 Nb 92.906	42 Mo 95.94	43 Tc (99)	44 Ru 101.07	45 Rh 102.905	46 Pd 106.4	47 Ag 107.870	48 Cd 112.40	49 In 114.82	50 Sn 118.69	51 Sb 121.75	52 Te 127.60	53 I 126.9044	54 Xe 131.30
6	55 Cs 132.905	56 Ba 137.34	57* La 138.91	72 Hf 178.149	73 Ta 180.948	74 W 183.85	75 Re 186.2	76 Os 190.2	77 Ir 192.2	78 Pt 195.09	79 Au 196.967	80 Hg 200.59	81 Tl 204.37	82 Pb 207.19	83 Bi 208.980	84 Po (210)	85 At (210)	86 Rn (222)
7	87 Fr (223)	88 Ra (226)	89† Ac (227)															

Rare Earth Elements→ 58-71

58 Ce 140.12	59 Pr 140.907	60 Nd 144.24	61 Pm (147)	62 Sm 150.35	63 Eu 151.96	64 Gd 157.25	65 Tb 158.924	66 Dy 162.50	67 Ho 164.930	68 Er 167.26	69 Tm 168.934	70 Yb 173.04	71 Lu 174.97

Actinide Series→ 90-103

90 Th (232.038)	91 Pa (231)	92 U (238.03)	93 Np (237)	94 Pu (242)	95 Am (243)	96 Cm (247)	97 Bk (247)	98 Cf (249)	99 Es (254)	100 Fm (253)	101 Md (256)	102 No (253?)	103 Lw (257)

cards. After some inspection, you realize that there are four varieties of cards—clubs, spades, hearts, and diamonds—and that each of the varieties has cards numbered 2 through 10. There are some unnumbered cards left over that appear to show faces of kings, queens, and knights in each of the four varieties.

You decide that the four cards that have a single club, spade, diamond, or heart in their center must stand for the number one. Thus you can arrange each of the varieties into a column of cards with numbers ranging in order from 1 through 10. The face cards could be placed in their proper columns according to some arbitrary rule. You might strongly suspect that the cards bearing a knight stood for an 11, those with a queen a 12, and finally the kings for a 13, since this is the usual pecking order in royal circles.

After arranging the cards in this way, you realize the pattern is disrupted here and there. There may be no 4 of diamonds where it seems one should be, and the king of clubs is missing, and so on. This was the situation that faced Mendeleyev when he had arranged his cards. He was sure that the disruptions in his pattern of cards represented elements that had not yet been found. Not only could he tell that an element was missing, but he even knew something of the properties of the missing element from the position it occupied in the pattern.

When Mendeleyev predicted in 1869 that certain elements with certain atomic masses and properties were yet to be found, he was greeted with cries of skepticism. But in 1875 when a new element, gallium, was discovered, with almost precisely the properties he had predicted, his skeptics became disciples. Mendeleyev became famous overnight, as well as a favorite of the czar. When Mendeleyev divorced his first wife and asked permission to marry a young art student, the Russian church was outraged, for it did not recognize divorce. But the czar consented. "Mendeleyev has two wives," said the czar, "but I have only one Mendeleyev."

In Chapter 11 we shall follow another development, called the eightfold way, which is strangely reminiscent of Mendeleyev's pattern of discovery and which led to the particles we now believe are the basic particles of nature. To get ready for these ultimate particles, we shall start our tour through the atom. There we shall find that Newton's "very strong attractions" had already been uncovered and were the very same forces that Maxwell used to form his theory of electromagnetic waves.

6

The Electron That Wasn't There

IT'S NOT a problem you are likely to meet, but suppose you wanted to look into a lion's mouth. You might consider various tactics: open its mouth while it's asleep; dangle a steak in front of its nose; tickle it to make it laugh. Probably none of these would seem worth pursuing. But then while you're trying to think of some other plan, the lion yawns, and you get a good look.

Something like this happened to the experimenters who were trying to see inside the atom. No plan seemed workable, and one by one all were discarded. And then the atom "yawned," but no one realized it at the time.

As usual, it all started with a misunderstanding. A French physicist, Henri Becquerel, was continuing studies begun by his father, also a physicist, on materials that absorb and reemit light—fluorescent materials. The green paint on watch faces that glow in the dark is an example. Becquerel had heard of the German physicist Wilhelm Roentgen's discovery of X rays. Roentgen believed that X rays were some kind of pulse or wave "in the aether [ether]" because, like light waves, they are not affected by magnetic or electrical forces. Becquerel wondered if his glowing materials might also emit X rays.

To test his theory, he took a small sample of a salt compound made from potassium and uranium atoms and placed it in bright sunlight. Much to his delight, the compound emitted radiation that penetrated the heavy protective paper on a photographic plate, fogging the film. He wanted to repeat the experiment, but some cloudy weather set in. So he placed his salt sample, along with a new film, in a drawer to await a sunnier day. A few days later he inadvertently developed the film, mistaking it for a different one, and to his considerable surprise discovered the unmistakable image of his salt sample. The salt had emitted radiation even though it had not been exposed to the sun. Becquerel had discovered what Madame Curie later named *radioactivity*. Unfortunately, his discovery lacked the dramatic appeal of X rays, which revealed bones inside a body. But, although Becquerel didn't know it, his atoms had yawned.

The uranium atoms in his salt sample were spontaneously spewing out penetrating particles and radiation. At first he thought the radiations were X rays because of their penetrating power. But then in 1899 he discovered that a part of the radiation was deflected when put in a magnetic field, demonstrating that this part, at least, was electrically charged. Democritus's hard, individual atoms could not have emitted anything. It was clear now that the atom had some kind of internal structure.

About the time that Becquerel was studying his fluorescent materials, an English physicist, J. J. Thomson, was studying the strange glow emitted by evacuated glass tubes through which an electric current passed (fig. 1). The glow seemed to be related to a stream of some kind of negatively charged material because the stream could be deflected by a magnet. After much experimenting, Thomson became convinced that the stream consisted of very small, very light, negatively charged particles. Later work revealed that his charged particles were *electrons*—one of the components of the atom.

In 1895 a young New Zealand scientist, Ernest Rutherford, arrived in England to become Thomson's first student. Thomson was so impressed with Rutherford that he gave him his highest recommendation

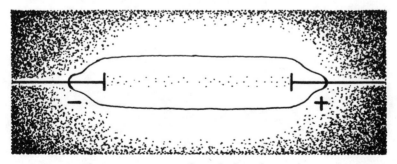

Fig. 1. Electrons streaming through the tube produce a glow.

Ernest Rutherford, circa 1906

for a physics professorship at McGill University in Montreal, Canada. There in 1899 Rutherford discovered that a part of Becquerel's emissions consisted of two kinds of particles. Rutherford called them *alpha* rays and *beta* rays. The alpha rays had a positive charge, and the beta rays a negative charge. The next year a French scientist discovered a third very energetic form of electromagnetic radiation, the *gamma* ray.

At the turn of the century, there was enough chemical and physical evidence to suggest that all atoms must contain electrons, since electrons could be produced from practically any substance in a number of different ways. Furthermore, since all evidence indicated that atoms are neutral, it was natural to assume that when an atom produced an electron—or perhaps electrons—what was left over must have a positive charge. A shadowy picture of the atom as some kind of mixture of positive and negative electric charges was emerging.

In 1904 Thomson proposed that the atom was a jellylike positive substance in which were embedded specks of negative charge—the electrons (fig. 2). As one might expect in England, this model of the atom came to be called the "raisin-pudding" model.

In 1907 Rutherford returned to England and began experiments

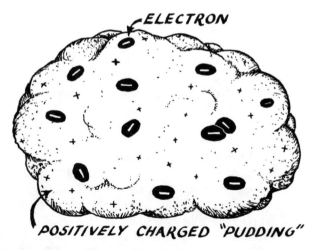

Fig. 2. In the raisin pudding model, electrons are embedded in a pudding of positive charge.

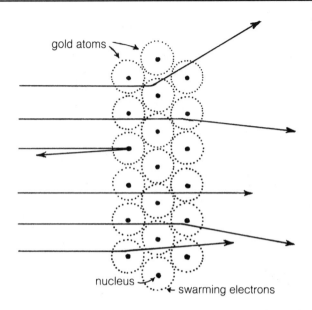

gold atoms

nucleus — swarming electrons

Fig. 3. Electrons bounce back when they hit the nucleus of a gold atom directly.

that revealed our present concept of the atom. By 1909 Becquerel had shown that beta rays were fast-moving electrons, and Rutherford had shown that alpha rays were positively charged particles with a mass about seventy-five hundred times as great as that of the electron. He planned to use alpha rays to probe the atom.

Rutherford and his colleagues placed a small speck of a radioactive substance, radium, at one end of a hollow lead tube. Alpha-ray "bullets" shot out the other end. Rutherford aimed his gun at a thin gold leaf, and behind the leaf he placed a zinc sulfide screen that would flash with a tiny pinpoint of light whenever an alpha particle struck it (fig. 3). He expected that most of the heavy alpha particles would pass through the gold leaf as though nothing were there. A few, however, would be slightly deflected if they happened to pass near or through the flimsy raisin-pudding gold atoms.

Just as expected, most of the alpha particles sailed through the gold leaf without deviation, and a few were deflected. Then Rutherford decided to look for alpha particles deflected back in the direction of the gun, fully expecting to find none. But after a few days of experiment-

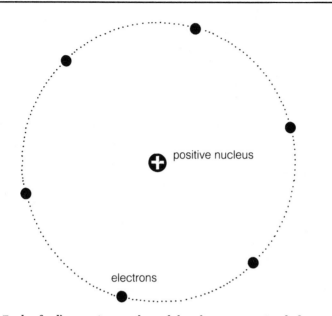

positive nucleus

electrons

Fig. 4. Rutherford's experiments showed that the atom consisted of a massive central core surrounded by electrons.

ing, an assistant rushed into Rutherford's office. "We have been able to get some alpha particles coming backwards," he said excitedly.

Rutherford was dumbfounded. "It was almost as incredible as if you fired a fifteen-inch shell at a piece of tissue paper and it came back and hit you," he said later. Obviously something was wrong with the raisin-pudding atom.

After careful analysis of the data, he decided that the atom consisted of a small dense center, which he called the *nucleus*, surrounded by swarming electrons (fig. 4). The nucleus, his data showed clearly, must not be more than one ten-thousandth the size of the atom itself, with a density about one million billion times the density of water. It was no wonder that the alpha particle bounced back when it occasionally collided with the dense nucleus of a gold atom.

Rutherford had come a long way from his early student-days description of the atom as ". . . a nice, hard fellow, red or grey in color according to taste." He received the Nobel Prize in 1908, and when he died he was buried in London's Westminster Abbey, just a few feet from Newton's tomb.

Our present concept of the atom is very near the one Rutherford proposed, and it accounts for the "very strong attraction" Newton imagined must exist to hold matter together. Any chunk of material—iron, for example—consists of a huge number of atoms, each with its swarm of electrons. When a number of iron atoms come together, each electron "feels" the electric and magnetic forces—the electromagnetic forces—generated by all of the nearby atoms. These forces cause the electrons to redistribute themselves, and on occasion an electron may even desert its parent atom to circulate around its parent and another atom (fig. 5). The net result of this redistribution is to form a strong bond among the iron atoms that is very stable and resistant to disruption. It is this electromagnetic "joining of hands" to provide a coherent whole—which an individual atom lacks—that holds the atoms together. Thus electromagnetism provides not only light waves, but also the "glue" that holds atoms together.

In spite of the great success of Rutherford's atom, he was well aware of one grave problem. His first scientific work in New Zealand

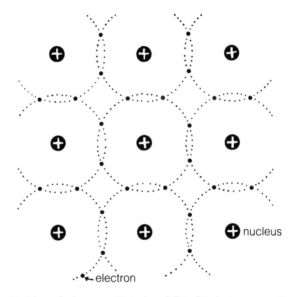

Fig. 5. Shared electrons "join hands" to bind atoms together.

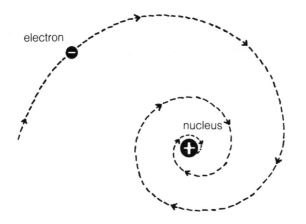

Fig. 6. According to Maxwell's equations, an orbiting electron should spiral into the atomic nucleus.

was with a low-frequency version of the electromagnetic waves predicted by Maxwell; today we call them *radio* waves. Maxwell's equations predict that radio waves could be generated by electric currents flowing back and forth in a piece of wire. Today we call such a device a *transmitting antenna*.

In a similar way, the electrons circling the nucleus of an atom should steadily radiate electromagnetic waves. If that were true, the negative electrons would gradually radiate away their energy and circle inward under the positive pull of the atom's nucleus (fig. 6). On their journey toward the nucleus, they would circle ever more rapidly; this, according to Maxwell's equations, means that the radiation they emit should increase continuously in frequency. In this picture, for example, the hydrogen electron would emit radiation with ever-increasing frequency until it plunged into the nucleus.

It's a clear picture, but unfortunately it's not what one observes when looking at the behavior of the hydrogen atom—or any other atom, for that matter. Observation shows emission at a particular frequency. In fact, the set of discrete emissions for any particular type of atom is one of the characteristics that tells us what kind of atom it is; it is a kind of fingerprint that allows astronomers to identify the atoms making up the stars by looking at their light.

Further investigation of the emissions from atoms showed that the radiation did not stream out continuously at one or more distinct frequencies, but in fact occurred in short bursts like bullets. This suggested that the emissions had something of the character of particles. The short bursts of energy at particular frequencies were named *photons*. Photons represent bundles of energy called *quanta*—from the Latin word meaning how much—because of their distinct nature. The amount of energy carried by a photon increases as the frequency of the associated emission increases. This was an important result worked out by Einstein—a result we shall need in our discussion of electrons and atoms in Chapter 8.

The idea that electromagnetic radiations—everything from light waves to radio waves to high-energy gamma rays—occur in fixed-energy bundles, or are *quantized*, suggests that matter in atoms may be restricted to certain energy levels. Niels Bohr, who didn't believe in horseshoes, took this idea to form a theory that for the first time explained the characteristic fingerprint emissions of the various atoms. His model of the atom is something like a miniature solar system, with a nucleus at the center and the electrons in various orbits circling the nucleus. His novel idea was that, like electromagnetic radiation, the energies of the electrons in the atom were constrained to certain fixed values. That is, the electrons had to circle the nucleus in certain orbits at fixed radii from the nucleus. In Bohr's theory, the electron dumped energy by jumping between allowable orbits (fig. 7).

His theory worked beautifully for simple atoms like the hydrogen atom, but it ran into trouble with more complicated atoms. And even more bothersome was the question, Why can the electrons circle the nucleus only in particular orbits? It was becoming obvious that Newton's laws, which worked so well for planets and apples, were failing at the atomic level, where both matter and radiation were quantized. And perhaps most puzzling of all, electromagnetic energy seemed to be both a wave and a particle—the photon—at the same time.

It was an exciting time for science, but the world was on the brink of a war that finally broke out in August of 1914. The great research laboratories were emptied as science and technology were directed toward the war effort. By the end of the war, in 1918, it appeared that Bohr's theory of the atom had run its course and something radically new was needed. In the years following the war, there was a great deal of experimentation with new ideas in many areas—architecture, music, the arts, theater, philosophy, and so on. In a

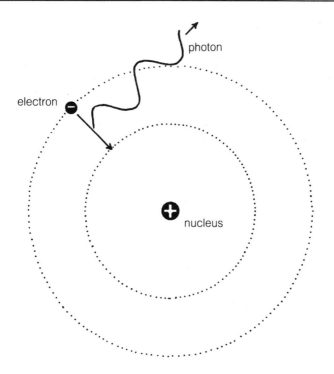

Fig. 7. In Bohr's model of the atom, photons are emitted when an electron jumps from an outer to an inner orbit.

world battered by the worst war in history, it seemed time to abandon old answers and search for new ones. The area of science was no exception.

As we have seen over and over, the ways of nature are not piece-meal; what seems to be true in one area is often true in others. Gravity applies to planets and golf balls, and electromagnetism to magnets and electrons. And so it was in 1923 that a French aristocrat, Prince Louis de Broglie, proposed—perhaps out of his sense of the symmetry of nature, conditioned by the general abandon of the times—that if waves could act like particles, then perhaps particles could act like waves. De Broglie even proposed a specific equation relating the mass of an object to its wavelength. He was guided here by some earlier work done by Einstein.

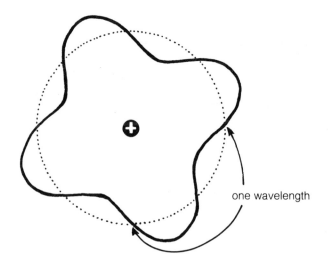

one wavelength

Fig. 8. In the de Broglie atom, the electron waves must surround the nucleus in whole numbers. Here we show a nucleus surrounded by four complete waves.

At the time de Broglie made his proposal, he really had no idea how the waviness of matter would manifest itself, or even what it meant for matter to be wavelike. Then in 1925 an American scientist, Clinton Davisson, accidentally discovered that electrons, under the right conditions, do indeed act like waves. He found that if he sent a beam of electrons through a piece of crystalline material, the electrons came out of the crystal in wave patterns. It was as though the electrons, while inside the crystal, interacted with each other like waves passing through a multilayered picket fence—exiting the fence in a pattern that depended on the size of the electron waves as well as the spacing between the pickets in the fence (fig. 8). In the crystal the "picket fence" is provided by the uniform arrangement of the atoms.

There was one more curious thing. The circumference of the smallest allowed electron orbit for the hydrogen atom was exactly equal to the wavelength of the electron predicted by de Broglie's equation, and the circumferences of the other allowed orbits were exact multiples of that wave length. Here appeared to be the explanation of the quantized energy states of the electron. If the circumferences of the orbits had to be whole numbers—fractional wavelengths were not allowed—then the allowed energies could not be fractional but had to correspond to the various whole-numbered orbits.

What was needed was a wave equation for matter just as Maxwell had found an equation for electromagnetic waves (fig. 8). The logjam was broken in 1925 and 1926. Two mathematical physicists, Erwin Schrödinger and Werner Heisenberg, working independently, each formulated a new approach to atomic motion that replaced Newton's laws of motion. It turned out that their approaches were mathematically equivalent, although this was a question of debate for some time. In addition, the new theory of matter waves collapsed into Newton's laws of motion for massive bodies; that is, Newton's laws are approximations that are exceedingly good as long as they aren't applied to objects with very small mass like atoms and electrons.

One of the most startling features of the new laws of atomic motion—*quantum mechanics* as the theory is called—was that it was no longer meaningful to talk about the exact position and the motion of a particle at the same time. The extent to which we can know position and motion at the same time depends on the mass of the object—the more massive the object, the better we can know its position and motion at the same time. For everyday objects, the mass is so great that our limitation on knowing both motion and position is very small—so small that we can't measure it. But for atoms and electrons, the limitation is very evident. How are we to understand this strange result?

This question, more than fifty years later, still generates much debate. One of the most satisfactory answers was given by Heisenberg. In the days before quantum mechanics, the world was divided into the observer and the observed—the astronomer turned his telescope on the stars, and the physicist measured the speed of falling objects. But when the objects are atoms and electrons, one has to consider carefully what it means to make measurements. A physicist watching a falling object is really seeing light from the object reflected into his eyes. As we know, light is particle-like; it exists as photons. So when it reflects off an object, there should be, according to Newton's third law, both an action and a reaction. In other words, the photon of light should disturb the object it bounces from. Usually that object is massive compared to the photon—mirrors don't move visibly when we shine a light on them.

But suppose the object is an electron. The very act of looking at

Fig. 9. Examining a small particle with a light moves the particle.

the electron—shining a light on it—significantly alters its position because its mass is so small. Now the observer and the observed are no longer disconnected; the act of observing alters the thing we are trying to observe (fig. 9).

On first thought it may seem that this is, at worst, an irritating feature of nature, but on second thought we see some profound implications. In Newton's world there were no surprises. Every event had its cause: The billiard ball strikes a cushion, which causes the ball to bounce off at a precise angle into another billiard ball; this causes both balls to take off in precisely determined new directions, and so on.

But suppose now the billiard balls are electrons. We take a flash picture to determine the electrons' locations. Now we know where the electrons were at the instant the picture was taken, but because of the flash, we don't know exactly where they are an instant after the flash. Without that knowledge, even if we knew what laws of motions to apply to electrons, we wouldn't be able to predict their exact locations at any point in the future because we don't know their starting positions exactly.

It might occur to us to use a weaker flash so as not to disturb the electrons so much, but that won't work because with a weaker flash we get a fuzzy picture. So we don't know the exact locations of the electrons at the moment of the flash, much less an instant later. For over fifty years, hundreds of experiments have demonstrated that there is no way around this problem. Newton's predictable universe is not a part of nature's plan.

The situation the creators of quantum mechanics faced was much like the one Newton and his followers faced: the equations work wonderfully well, but what do they mean? While the young theorists were working out the implications of quantum mechanics, the now somewhat older Niels Bohr struggled to find a deeper meaning in the equations. As a young man he had been influenced by Denmark's most prominant philosopher, Soren Kierkegaard. Kierkegaard believed that reality did not have an existence independent of man's attempt to understand it; reality, he believed, is changed by the very act of contemplating it.

Bohr applied Kierkegaard's idea to the physical world in what came to be known as the Copenhagen interpretation of quantum mechanics. In this view the more we insist on knowing about the world *now*, the less we shall know about its future. Deep inspection of the world upsets the present arrangement. In the real world we must compromise between knowing everything about now and knowing something about the future. Bohr further believed that atoms and electrons are creations of men's mind in an attempt to bring some order into the microscopic chaos. There are not atoms and electrons— only observations, Bohr said.

Albert Einstein never did believe that quantum mechanics was a complete theory. He believed that a more adequate theory would not prevent one from knowing in detail the future course of events.

In the next chapter we shall see how Einstein, again with relativity theory, finally settled the ether problem.

Niels Bohr

7

It's All Relative

BY THE MIDDLE of the 1920s, quantum mechanics had shown that the observer and the observed cannot be separated. This was a great change from the Newtonian view that the universe was a vast stage whose drama was viewed unperturbed by man. According to quantum mechanics, the audience and the unfolding drama are intertwined; the play is altered by the audience during the production. Newton's concept of absolute time and space didn't fit into the new ideas that included observers as part of the picture. To understand this intertwining, we need to consider once more a problem with which we are now familiar—ether. The ether, presumably, was at rest with respect to absolute space, and light waves were a ripple in the ether.

In 1879 Maxwell wrote a letter to a young naval officer, Albert A. Michelson, who was assigned to the Nautical Almanac Office in Washington, D.C. Maxwell suggested an experiment he believed would reveal the elusive ether. He based his suggestion on a simple idea: A rock dropped into a pool of water causes ripples that travel in concentric circles, at a particular speed, from the point where the rock hits the water. One could measure this speed by noting the time it took a particular ripple to travel a known distance.

Let's suppose that we were in a boat traveling toward the center of the ripples (fig. 1). It would appear to us that the ripples were approaching the boat at a speed greater than the speed measured by a person in a stationary boat. To us, in the moving boat, the apparent speed of the ripples would be the speed of the boat plus the speed of the ripples.

In his letter to Michelson, Maxwell suggested that since the earth moves about 30 kilometers per second in its motion about the sun, it is in fact moving through the ether. The idea was to measure this movement with a suitable arrangement of mirrors and light signals. The earth played the part of the moving boat, and the ether was the water through which the ripples—the light waves—traveled. Thus as the earth moves through the ether, the speed of the light waves should change as the earth changes its direction of motion about the sun, just as the speed of waves hitting a boat changes as the boat changes its direction of motion through the waves.

One problem with this arrangement is that the sun itself might also be moving through the ether. But if the measurements were made throughout the year, when the earth is at different points in its orbit about the sun, the sun's motion through the ether would cancel out. In Michelson's particular arrangement of mirrors and light signals, he should have found different values for the speed of light, depending on whether the signal was traveling *with* the direction of the earth or *across* it.

What Michelson found, to his astonishment, was that the speed of light was always the same, whether he measured in the same direction as the earth's motion or across it. It was as though the person in the moving boat and the one in the boat at rest concluded that the ripples had the same speed.

Fig. 1. The measured speed of the waves depends on the boat's motion.

More tests gave the same result. Michelson became America's first Nobel Prize winner for discovering something that wasn't there.

In 1905 the Gettysburg Address of science papers appeared. It was short, easy to understand, and beautifully written. It said in part, "The introduction of a 'luminiferous aether' will prove to be superfluous, inasmuch as the view here to be developed will not require an 'absolute stationary space.'" The author was Albert Einstein, age twenty-six, a minor clerk in the Swiss patent office in Berne.

Einstein was born in 1879, the year Maxwell died. He was an indifferent student and left school in his mid-teens at the request of the principal, who told him that his presence in the class undermined discipline. After spending a year wandering around northern Italy, he applied and was finally admitted to an engineering school in Zurich. His school friends remembered him as charming, witty, and at times brilliant; they recalled that he spent more time in cafes than in lectures. Much to the relief of his family and professors, he graduated in 1900.

Discouraged and full of self-doubt after a long, fruitless search for employment, he welcomed the clerical job he obtained at the Swiss patent office through the help of a friend. He remarked years later that he was fortunate to have got the patent-office job because, unlike his fellow graduates, he was not under pressure to pursue work his superiors thought important and had freedom to follow his own inclinations.

The 1905 paper, titled "On the Electrodynamics of Moving Bodies," was based on two simple but extraordinary ideas. The first was that all the laws of physics, not just some of them, are the same for all observers moving in uniform motion relative to each other. In other words, if there is no acceleration, the laws of physics are the same for all observers. In effect Einstein said that the idea of absolute space is wrong. It can't be observed, and assuming its existence doesn't lead to any useful result, so there is no point in talking about it any more—another example of Ockham's razor. Of course, abolishing absolute space also did away with the ether. Light waves were now seen as self-sustaining waves with no need to propagate in anything. The reality was the light wave itself, not some disturbance passing through the ether. Einstein's first statement is really a reaffirmation of Newton's statement that the laws of nature should be identical in inertial frames of reference.

The second idea simply stated what Michelson had observed: the speed of light is the same in all directions for all observers in

Albert Einstein when he was a clerk at the Berne (Switzerland) Patent Office.

inertial frames of reference. This means that whatever form the laws of physics take, they must not violate this rule. Furthermore, no material object may travel faster than the speed of light.

Now we can readily see one problem with Newton's world of absolute time and space: if two jet planes approach each other at 1,000 miles per hour, their relative speed is 2,000 miles per hour. But if one plane is moving at the speed of light and the other at 1,000 miles per hour, their relative speed, in Newton's world, is the speed of light plus 1,000 miles per hour. In Einstein's world, however, their relative speed is the speed of light, since this is the highest speed nature allows.

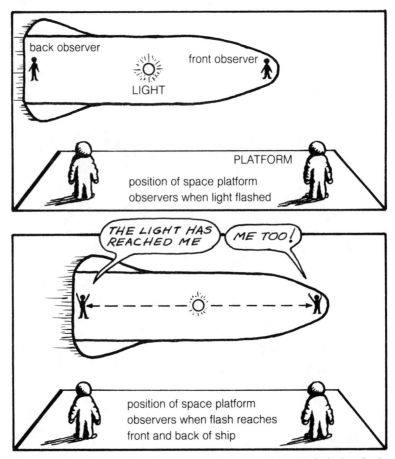

Fig. 2A. According to the observers in the space ship, the light hits both ends of the space ship at the same time.

Einstein was so convinced of the truth of this idea that he was willing to turn man's intuitive notions about space and time upside down so that the laws of physics did not allow speeds faster than the speed of light. According to Einstein, the only thing that can travel at the speed of light is light itself. We cannot accelerate any material object to the speed of light, no matter how hard we push it. "If we are to understand the universe," he said, "we must free ourselves from the prejudices of our five senses. What we see, hear, and touch can fool us."

Let's see if we can understand how altering our concepts of space and time can accommodate Einstein's strange results. We shall assume that his two ideas are correct and then follow the consequences.

Imagine a spaceship passing a space platform in outer space. Observers are stationed at the two ends of the spaceship, and two more are on the space platform, as shown in figure 2A. A light in the exact center of the spaceship flashes on for an instant, sending a pulse of light toward the two ends of the ship.

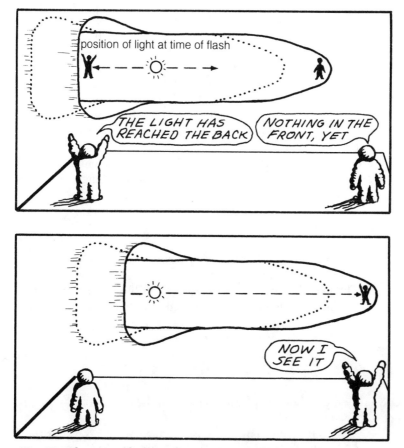

Fig. 2B. The space platform observers say the light hits the back of the space ship first and then the front.

According to Einstein, the light travels at the same speed in both directions through the spaceship. So the two observers in the ship see the flash arrive at the two ends at the same time. Would the observers on the platform agree?

Let's imagine that the observers on the platform are positioned so that when the flash arrives at the front of the ship, one of the observers on the platform is exactly opposite the observer in the front of the ship, and the other observer on the platform is exactly opposite the observer in the back of the ship. Now the two observers at the back—one in the spaceship and the other on the platform—would agree as to when the flash arrived at the rear of the ship. And similarly, the two observers at the front would agree as to when the flash arrived at the front. But what would the two observers on the platform say about the moment the flash reached the two ends of the ship?

From their point of view, the spaceship is moving so that the rear of the ship is *approaching* the light pulse, while the front is moving *away from* the light pulse. In other words, the pulse reaches the rear of the spaceship before it reaches the front because the distances traveled in the two directions are different. Furthermore, as figure 2B shows, the two observers on the platform were not equidistant from the flash at the instant of the flash; the one watching the back of the ship is closer to the flash than is the one watching the front of the ship. Obviously then, the flash could not have reached the two ends of the spaceship at the same time.

Let's summarize these observations:

1. The observers in the spaceship say the flash hits the two ends of the ship at the same time.
2. The two observers at the back—one in the ship and the other on the platform—agree on the time the flash reaches the rear of the ship, and the two observers at the front agree on when the flash reaches the front of the ship.
3. The observers on the platform say the flash hit first the back of the ship and then the front.

Obviously these three conclusions cannot all be true at once—at least not in Newtonian time.

Because the conclusions are so contradictory, let's consider them once more in different words: If the two observers standing side by side at the front agree that they saw the flash at the same time, and

Fig. 3A. The space ship observers see the light pulse bouncing back and forth over the shortest path.

the two rear observers standing side by side agree that they saw the flash at the same time, then we can't have the two observers on the space platform insisting that the pulses hit at different times—not if time is the same for all observers.

But if Einstein is correct, we must conclude that only observers at the same location agree on when things happen, while those in relative uniform motion watching events separated in distance will not agree. The time when events separated by distance occur is *relative*, according to the observers' motion—not absolute as Newton believed. If light moves at the same speed for all observers, there is no alternative but to conclude that the flow of time is not the same for everyone.

Let's consider now in a little more detail how the flow of time differs for observers moving relative to one another. We return to our spaceship and platform and consider how two clocks—one on the spaceship and the other on the platform—keep time. As figure 3A shows, the clocks are very simple. Each consists of two mirrors, placed parallel to each other and parallel to the spaceship's direction of motion, with a pulse of light bouncing back and forth between the two mirrors. We shall say that a pulse of light bouncing back and forth once equals one "tick." And we'll assume that the mirrors in each clock are separated by the same distance, so that if the clocks sat motionless, side by side, they would tick at the same rate.

Now an interesting question arises: What does an observer in the spaceship say about the ticking rate of the clock on the platform? And similarly, what does an observer on the platform say about the spaceship's clock?

As figure 3B shows, it appears to both observers that the pulse of light in the other's clock travels a greater distance as it bounces back and forth. That is, each observer says the other's clock ticks more slowly than his own. As the relative speed between the two observers increases, the apparent length of the path of the tick increases accordingly. Thus each observer says that the other's clock runs more and more slowly as the relative speed increases. There is no other possible conclusion if the speed of light is the same for all observers. And as strange as this result seems, very accurate clocks carried in rockets do demonstrate this slowing of time.

Now—if time is not the same for all observers, neither is space. We can see this by returning once again to our spaceship and platform and the light pulse in the center of the spaceship. The observers in the spaceship would say that they were standing one spaceship length apart when the flash reached the two ends of their ship. And they

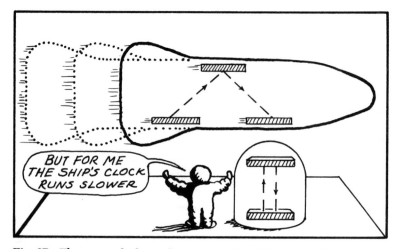

Fig. 3B. The space platform observers see the light pulse taking a longer path.

would also say that the two observers on the platform were standing exactly opposite the ends of the spaceship when the flash reached the ends. But the observers on the platform, as figure 3B shows, would not agree. From their point of view, the flash reached the rear before it reached the front. Furthermore, the spaceship moved in the meantime; to be at opposite ends of the spaceship at the same time, they would have to stand closer together. In other words, they believe the spaceship is shorter than their separation on the platform.

From Einstein's first idea, that all observers have equal validity, we could argue that it is the space platform that is moving, and that therefore it is the platform that is shortened, not the spaceship. So we come to the conclusion that moving objects are shortened in the direction of motion, with both sets of observers insisting with equal validity that it is they who are at rest while the others move.

If we review these arguments, we realize that both the slowing of time and the contraction of space are based on arguments having to do with simultaneity of events separated in distance. In other words, space and time are intertwined, and how they are related depends on the observer. Thus the absolute separation of space and time in Newton's universe is collapsed into an integrated whole we call *space-time*. Just as Maxwell reduced electricity and magnetism to electro-magnetism, so Einstein reduced space and time to spacetime, providing another economy in our understanding of the universe. Furthermore, since any observer is just as valid as any other observer, there is complete symmetry among observers. There is no privileged frame of reference anchored firmly to a universe-pervading ether. We see Ockham's razor and Greek symmetry at work again.

It is important to emphasize that it is not a case of clocks running slow or objects shrinking in Newton's absolute time and space, but rather spacetime itself that alters according to the observer's point of view. Therefore, any objects embedded in spacetime must change accordingly. We see now how Einstein's two apparently simple ideas have completely changed our whole concept of the nature of space and time.

Although Einstein's ideas still seem strange some eighty years after they were first proposed, any person who thought deeply about the problem of simultaneity centuries before Einstein might have realized that something was wrong with Newton's absolute space and time. Let's imagine we are back on the space platform watching two space ships. One heads directly toward our platform, and the other moves across the oncoming spaceship's path on a collision course (fig. 4). The captain on the oncoming spaceship, seeing the collision ahead, takes evasive action and avoids the collision.

Now let's consider this event from our space platform perspective. We see both spaceships from light that is reflected from them back into our eyes. We'll imagine this light is provided by powerful beacons on our platform. In Newton's world, the light reaching us from the oncoming spaceship travels with the speed of light plus the spaceship's speed, while the light from the spaceship crossing the path reaches us with only the speed of light, since that ship is moving parallel to us and not toward us. That is, the image of the oncoming ship reaches us before the image of the passing ship, so that the relative positions of the ships are different for us from what they are for the captain of the oncoming ship. From our point of view, we see the oncoming ship take evasive action for no apparent reason.

Can it be that what appears a potential collision to the captain is not a potential collision for us? This is the conclusion we must reach if we believe Newton. But there is not the slightest evidence that an event for one observer is a nonevent for another. If a bomb blows up on the ground, it blows up for all observers, whether they are watching it from a high-speed plane or from a protective barrier anchored to the earth. But the time at which the bomb explodes may be different for different observers watching different clocks—as predicted by Einstein.

It appears from Einstein's papers that just such considerations as these would have led him to revise absolute space and time into spacetime even if Michelson had never conducted his experiment. Such is the power of the careful examination of seemingly ordinary events.

Perhaps the most curious and awesome product of spacetime is the most famous formula of our century: $E = mc^2$—the formula behind the atomic bomb. This is the formula that says that mass, m, can be converted to energy, E—or conversely, energy can be turned into mass. And what is c? It's the speed of light. Thus we see that the speed of light plays the role of a number that tells us how energy and mass are related. It is also one of those invariants that scientists are always looking for. The reason so much energy can be obtained from so little mass is that c is such a large number—185,000 miles per second. And c^2 means c times c, a much larger number—34,596,000,000.

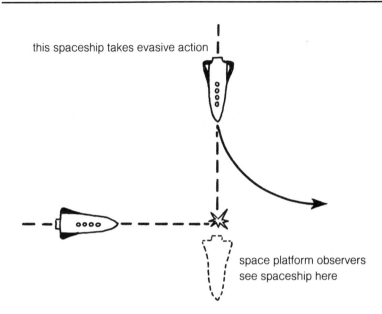

this spaceship takes evasive action

space platform observers
see spaceship here

space platform

Fig. 4. The captain of the space ship approaching the space platform sees a collision ahead, while the space platform observers do not understand why the captain takes evasive action.

How is $E = mc^2$ a product of spacetime? We recall that only light can travel at the speed of light, and that any material object, such as a baseball or an atom, can come as close to the speed of light as we wish but cannot reach it. As the object's speed approaches the speed of light, each small increase in speed requires ever more energy, and to reach the speed of light itself requires infinite energy—an obvious impossibility.

Let's return now to Newton's second law: force equals mass times acceleration, or $f = ma$. As we know, this law means that if a force, f, acts on a mass, m, it will accelerate with a constant rate, a. This means that if the force acts long enough, it will continuously accelerate the mass until it reaches the speed of light—an impossibility. The only conclusion is that the mass, m, increases with the speed of the object, so that our constant force, f, produces ever decreasing acceleration as the object's speed increases.

We can see this more clearly if we rewrite $f = ma$ as $a = f/m$. Here we easily see that as mass increases, the acceleration gets ever smaller, since the force always has a constant value.

Now the moving energy of an object—*kinetic* energy, as it is called—depends on the speed of an object and its mass. At last we begin to see what is happening. The energy that we expend on pushing the object with constant force goes into increasing both the object's speed and its mass. At low speeds the most visible result of the pushing is that the object's speed increases, but as the object approaches the speed of light, its mass begins to increase rapidly at a rate that keeps it from reaching the speed of light no matter how long it is pushed. In other words, here is a way of converting energy into mass.

In the atomic bomb or a nuclear power plant, the process works in reverse: Mass is turned into energy. But even in more ordinary situations, this effect operates—it's just that the result is less dramatic. In a fire that provides energy in the form of heat, the combustion products made by the fuel combining with oxygen are lighter than the original fuel and oxygen. The difference, however, is very, very small. If we contained the fire in an insulated box, so that no heat or combustion products escaped, we would find that the box and its contents weighed the same before and after the burning—another indication that mass and energy are interchangeable.

All this brings us to something we said in Chapter 4, that mass is an invariant quantity. Now we see that we must modify that statement to say that it is the sum of mass and energy that remains the same, that is invariant. In the example of the fire in the box, we see an example of this mass-energy invariance. The box and its contents weigh the same before and after the fire. Initially the weight of the material in the box is due to the fuel and oxygen, and after the fire it is due to the combustion products and the weight of the heat energy.

The ideas we have discussed here illustrate what has come to be called Einstein's *Special Theory of Relativity*. It is called the special theory because it contains no reference to gravity, which the *General Theory of Relativity* does. We shall have more to say about the General Theory in Chapter 9, but as we shall see in the next chapter, it was the Special Theory, without gravity, that helped guide de Broglie in his formulation of matter waves.

8

The Ghost in the Electron

IN CHAPTER 6 we learned that Prince Louis de Broglie suggested that particles could perhaps be wavelike, and in 1923 he proposed an equation that related the mass of an object to its wavelength. He was guided in this proposal by Einstein's work—particularly from $E = mc^2$, from the Special Theory of Relativity, and from Einstein's proposal that light comes in packets called photons.

We remember that Einstein said that the energy of a photon is related to the frequency of the light associated with the photon. This relationship turns out to be very simple. To find the energy of a photon, we simply multiply its frequency by a number called Planck's constant. That is, the energy of the photon, E, is given by $E = hf$, where h is Planck's constant and f is the frequency of the radiation. Like the velocity of light (c), h is another invariant number in nature, named for Max Planck, the German physicist who discovered it. And h is similar to c in another way: as c relates energy to mass via the equation $E = mc^2$, so h relates electromagnetic energy to frequency via the equation $E = hf$.

This is very suggestive. If energy is related to mass, and energy is related to frequency, then it seems plausible that frequency is related to mass via the common denominator, energy. But since frequency and wavelength are related—for a wave moving at a constant speed, the wavelength decreases with the increasing frequency—we can extend the mass-frequency relation to a mass-wavelength relation, which was de Broglie's original suggestion.

Let's return to our "picket fence" in the crystal, discussed in Chapter 6. There we learned that an American scientist discovered that electrons passing through crystalline material interfere with each other as though they are wavelike—as de Broglie proposed. We shall consider that experiment again, but with a much simpler arrangement. We'll replace the picket fence with a solid fence that has two boards missing, as shown in figure 1. Let's suppose that the fence runs along the side of a building that is a few yards inside the fence and that we stand on the other side of the fence throwing baseballs in random directions at the fence. These are special baseballs covered with a dye, so that when a ball passes through a space left by a missing board, it hits the building and leaves a mark on the wall.

If we threw a great number of baseballs, we would expect to see a concentration of marks on the wall directly behind the two spaces, but there would be a few marks on either side of the areas of greatest concentration because some balls would not pass squarely through a space but would bounce off the edges of the boards on either side of the space. The figure shows the distribution of marks we would expect.

Let's consider now the kind of distribution we would expect from a wavelike substance passing through the slots. Suppose a water main

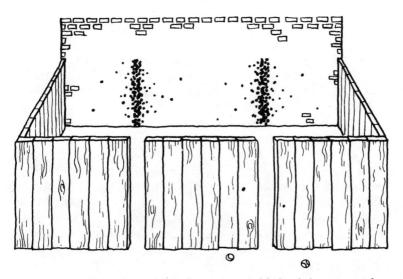

Fig. 1. The ball-marks on the wall are clustered behind the missing slats.

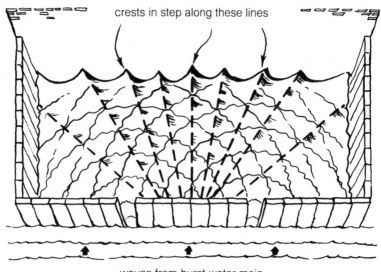

crests in step along these lines

waves from burst water main

Fig. 2. **The waves recombine behind the fence to form patterns of maximum and minimum wave height.**

bursts, sending a steady flow of water toward the fence. Small uniform waves develop. We'll consider a particular wave crest that reaches both slots in the fence at the same time, as shown in figure 2. As the crest passes through the slots, circular wave patterns emerge on the other side of the fence, as the figure shows. These two patterns interfere with each other so that at a point in time and space where the two patterns meet crest to crest, a new wave with twice the height of either of the original waves is formed. At points in time and space where a trough and a crest meet, the wave height is small or zero. As the figure shows, all the points along a line extending away from the fence and midway between the two slots represent positions where the wave crests meet in step to produce a maximum-height wave pattern. As we move away from this line, the circular patterns begin to meet out of step, finally producing little or no wave. And farther on again the waves meet in step, producing a maximum wave, and so on.

Suppose now we replace our fence with a miniature fence with two very narrow slots, and our baseballs with electrons. We imagine that some device, perhaps something like a hot element in an electric light bulb, boils out electrons in random directions, some of which head for the miniature fence. Behind the fence we replace the wall with a special screen that records a permanent dot at each point where an electron hits it.

If we leave our electron-generating device on long enough, a pattern of dots will build up on the screen, giving us the distribution of electron impacts. If electrons are small particles, something like miniature baseballs, then we would expect to see two concentrated regions of impact, one behind each of the two slots, similar to the distribution pattern in figure 1.

But when this experiment is performed, this is not what the observers find. Instead they find an impact distribution similar to the distribution of waves as shown in figure 2!

What is even more curious, if we "turn down" our electron source so that it generates only one electron at a time, we still get the same wave impact pattern on the screen. That is, we see a new dot appear here and there on the screen, one after another, building up a wave pattern. If an electron is like a baseball, it goes through either one slot or the other, but the wave pattern on the screen says this cannot be the case. It is as though each electron somehow goes through *both* slots, interferes with itself as it emerges from the other side, and builds up the observed pattern.

At this point it might occur to us to do something interesting: Cover up one of the slots, and see what pattern emerges. If we do this we find there's a maximum concentration of dots just behind the uncovered slot, with the concentration trailing off symmetrically on either side. This is like the distribution we would expect if we threw baseballs at a fence with only one board missing.

So we come to an astounding conclusion: An electron passing through a slot "knows" whether there is another slot or not. Yet more astounding, even when the slots are very far apart, perhaps thousands of miles, we would still get wavelike patterns on the screen! The electron is affected by the slot it didn't go through no matter how far away the slot is. The electron, like a ghost, is everywhere and nowhere when it passes through the slots, only to materialize later as a dot on the screen.

In Chapter 6 we learned about the search for a wave equation that would apply to de Broglie's matter waves. Of the two men most responsible for the early development of quantum mechanics, Schrö-dinger and Heisenberg, whom we met in Chapter 6, Schrödinger's approach was the one that led to an equation for matter waves. At first Schrödinger believed that the matter waves in his equation repre-sented some kind of "smeared-out" electron, or a smeared-out version of any other small particle to which the equation was applied. But it was hard to imagine matter smeared out in space only to materialize finally at a particular point in space as the electron did when it left a mark on the screen.

Many experiments have shown that an electron is an object with a definite mass and size too small to measure. That is still true today. After much discussion and thought, a new interpretation of the matter waves developed. In this interpretation the wave does not represent a smeared-out particle, but rather the probability that the particle is at a particular location. Let's apply this idea to the two-slotted fence.

When an electron heads toward the fence, emerges on the other side, and hits the screen, there is no way to know exactly what path it took until it hits. The best we can do is to say that its most *probable* path is such and such, and other paths, although less likely, are nonethe-less possible. If we apply the matter-wave equation to the two-slotted fence, it predicts precisely the observed wavelike distribution pattern. The equation does not tell us which path a particular electron takes— it tells us only that after enough electrons have passed through the slots, a wavelike distribution pattern emerges.

What happens between the time the electron leaves the generating source and the time it hits the screen we shall never know. Like discussing ether, which finally proved to be of no use, talking about the path of the electron is a waste of time. Nature simply will not engage in that dialogue with us. In some sense, the electron does not even exist until we detect its location on the screen. And here again we see the performer and the audience bound together.

Erwin Schrödinger was very unhappy with this interpretation of his matter-wave equation, and he said at one point that he was sorry he had ever considered the problem if this was to be the resolution. To emphasize his displeasure, he concocted a story about a cat trapped in a sealed box. The box contained a very small amount of radioactive material—not enough to harm the cat. The cat's danger lay in the fact that the box also contained a small glass bottle of poisonous gas and a hammer mechanism that could be triggered by the radioactive material; if the radioactive material emitted some sort of radiation,

Fig. 3. There is a fifty-fifty chance that the poisonous gas will be released, killing the cat.

the hammer mechanism would be tripped, breaking the bottle, releasing the gas, and killing the cat (fig. 3).

Suppose, said Schrödinger, there is a fifty-fifty chance that the material will emit radiation in an interval of one minute. According to our conventional way of thinking, if we looked inside the box after one minute we would expect to find the cat either dead or alive. If the cat was dead, we would say it had died sometime earlier because the gas had been released.

But this, said Schrödinger, was not the correct way to view the situation if the probabilistic interpretation of his matter-wave equation was correct. The matter waves represent what *might* happen, and until the electron hits the screen or the box is opened, we can only speculate about the past. According to Schrödinger's story, the cat is neither alive nor dead until we open the box. It is the act of opening the box, or making an observation, that provides a dead cat or a live one. According to quantum mechanics, before the box is opened all we can say is that there are two matter waves, one representing a live cat and the other a dead cat, existing at the same time. And when we open the box, we get one of two possibilities, with equal probability (fig. 4).

Today most physicists don't believe that Schrödinger's cat-in-the-

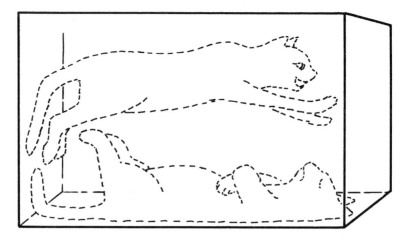

Fig. 4. Before the box is opened there are matter waves for both the live cat and the dead cat.

box example can be analyzed correctly along the lines Schrödinger laid out, but the story does highlight Bohr's statement that there are not atoms and electrons, only observations. Newton's objective reality, where objects have a unique identity independent of the observer, is apparently not part of the microscopic and submicroscopic world. As the American Nobel Prize-winning physicist Richard Feynman said, ". . . it is safe to say that no one understands quantum mechanics. Do not keep saying to yourself . . . 'how can it possibly be like that?' . . . Nobody knows how it can be like that."

Today's scientists are in much the same position that natural philosophers were in Newton's day. Newton's theory worked amazingly well, but the strange gravitational force that reached across the universe was incomprehensible. Similarly, quantum mechanics is one of the most successful theories we have, and yet its workings are so far removed from our everyday experiences that we really can't comprehend it.

Einstein was squarely in the Newtonian camp that says there is a real, objective world "out there" with a definite character independent of any observer. On one occasion he said to a younger colleague with whom he was arguing, "Do you really believe the moon exists only when you look at it?"

In 1935 Einstein, Boris Podolsky, and Nathan Rosen published a famous paper now called "The EPR Paper." In essence it said that quantum mechanics is not a complete description of physical reality. The arguments in The EPR Paper are technical, but we can get the idea of what is involved by considering the following situation.

Suppose you have two identical coins in your hand and you give one of them to a friend who is leaving on an airplane for a city two thousand miles away. After your friend has arrived in the distant city, you call him on the phone and explain that you wish to do an experiment. You are going to flip your coin to see whether it comes up heads or tails, and he is to do the same after you have made your flip. Then you will compare notes, telling each other how your coins turned up.

Your friend is a frequent visitor to your city, and each time he returns you hand him one of two identical coins. In this way you are able to conduct the experiment many times. After a while you begin to notice something very remarkable: Every time your coin turns up heads, his turns up tails, and vice versa.

In the Newtonian world, you expect to find no detailed relation whatever between the results you obtained and those of your friend. Each of you would find that your coins turned up randomly heads or tails about half the time. If you compared notes in detail, you'd find that sometimes when you had a head he had a tail, other times when he had a head you had a tail, and sometimes you both came up with heads or tails.

But in the world of quantum mechanics, this is not what happens. Here the result would be more like this: Whenever your coin came up heads, your friend's came up tails; and whenever yours came up tails, his came up heads. This suggests that your friend is cheating. Somehow he knows the result of your coin flip before you tell him, and he somehow throws his coin to make it come up the opposite of yours. You might suspect that someone is secretly watching you and telephoning the result of your flips to your friend.

Now we know from Special Relativity that no signal can travel faster than the speed of light. This limit gives you an idea. Since your friend is two thousand miles away, it takes a small but definite time for any message to reach him. So you plan the experiment so that he has to flip his coin immediately after you flip yours, before any message could reach him. Much to your dismay, with this new arrangement his coin still comes up opposite to yours.

You try a new experiment. You tell your friend to take a new coin from his pocket and use it instead of the one you gave him as he boarded the plane. Now you find that the coins come up randomly, as you expected in the first place. The only difference in the two experiments seems to be that the pairs of coins used in the first experiment had been together at one time, whereas those in the second experiment had never been together.

This bizarre behavior is the kind of behavior predicted by quantum mechanics. Quantum mechanics says that the first two coins, since they had been together at one time, should be considered as twin components of a two-coin system that are somehow connected no matter how far apart they may be. What you do to either coin affects the total two-coin system.

In terms of matter waves, there is not one matter wave for each of the two coins; instead there is one composite matter wave representing the two-coin system. On the other hand, the two coins in the second experiment are not part of a two-coin system, since they had never been together. So they are at liberty to act independently of each other because each is represented by a different matter wave. Of course, the description we have just given does not apply to coins because they are much too massive, but it does give the flavor of how elementary particles act if they were at one time together.

Quantum mechanics seems to say that a measurement taken at one location can instantaneously affect a measurement taken at another. In The EPR Paper it was this instantaneous connection that bothered the authors most. It appeared to violate the idea that no object or message can travel faster than the speed of light.

Einstein did not question the result of the experiment with the "coins," or atoms, that had been together; there was too much evidence that the result was correct. What he did question was the completeness of quantum mechanics. He felt that a complete theory would account for the strange behavior. Since he ruled out the possibility of instantaneous connection, he decided that in some unknown way when the two "coins" were together they conspired to produce the bizarre result. It was as though the coin that was thrown first said to the other coin, "Let's play a trick on the two friends. No matter how I am flipped I will manage to fall first heads, then tails, then tails, then heads, and so forth. You memorize my heads-tails sequence, and then you can fall each time exactly opposite to the way I fall."

Einstein felt that a complete version of quantum mechanics would expose this trick, or something akin to it. In other words, the two coins, because they had been together at one time, could each carry away the necessary information to account for the curious results. Theories as to where the coins carry information have come to be called hidden variable theories.

In 1964 John S. Bell, of the European Organization for Nuclear Research, showed that it was possible to decide experimentally between Einstein's fuller theory with its hidden variables and ordinary quantum mechanics. Since that time a number of different but conclusive experiments have been performed, and the verdict is in: Einstein is wrong, and ordinary quantum mechanics is right.

What are we to make of these strange results and their interpretation? Perhaps we can put the situation in better perspective by returning to Schrödinger's cat. Suppose we have no idea what is inside the box and further that nature forbids us from ever looking inside. All we know is that, whenever we put a cat in the box, it comes out dead or alive with equal probability. This is simply an observation involving no theory or interpretation of a theory. This part of our study corresponds to observing the coins coming up randomly but always with opposite sides, at the two locations.

After thinking about the observations for a while, we might propose a mathematical theory that predicts the cat will be found dead or alive with equal probability. If it is a good theory, it will predict results that go beyond what we have observed. Perhaps our theory predicts that only black cats die with fifty-fifty probability, whereas white cats never die. We try the experiment and, much to our gratification—and the white cats' as well—the prediction turns out true. This gives us much greater confidence in our theory. We now have a theory, like quantum mechanics, that holds for all of our observations.

But then we begin to wonder what is in the box. We know our theory works perfectly well, but we are dissatisfied because we want to know the "reality" behind our theory. We are like Newton's contemporaries who were amazed by the accuracy of his theory of gravitation but couldn't help wondering about the mysterious gravitational force that permeated the universe.

It seems clear that something in the box is killing black cats. We might even speculate that it is something like the hammer–poison gas mechanism proposed by Schrödinger. But we would have to add the stipulation that the gas killed only black cats, not white cats. Someone else might suggest that the box contains a black-cat aging

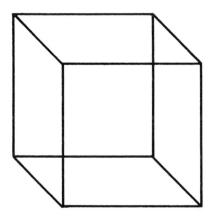

Fig. 5. The cube appears to change its orientation.

machine so that half the black cats die of old age before the box is opened. There are, of course, any number of interpretations we might suggest—some perhaps more satisfying than others—but ultimately we are resigned to the fact that, since nature will never let us see inside the box, we will never know which interpretation, if any, is correct.

There have been many interpretations of quantum mechanics. One says that ordinary language needs to be altered when we apply it to the submicroscopic world. Words like "either" and "or" need to be given new meanings so that when we talk about the electron going through "either" this opening in the fence "or" that one, we are not surprised by the wave interference pattern that appears on the other side of the fence. Niels Bohr summarized the difficulty of using words in situations where they don't apply with a typical Bohr story: A small boy enters a candy store and asks for two pennies' worth of mixed candy. The storekeeper, smiling, hands the boy two gumdrops and says, "Here's your candy. You do the mixing." The idea of mixing two pieces of candy is both amusing and nonsensical.

Redefining words so that quantum mechanics doesn't seem so mysterious strikes most people as simply sweeping the problem under the rug. After all, the observations are still just as mysterious, and we have only obscured that fact with language. Ordinary language has evolved to serve us in our everyday lives, and to change it shifts the mystery from the submicroscopic world to the world of ordinary experience.

If we insist, as Einstein did, that there is really a "there" out there, then we have this peculiar connection between objects once together but now separated. But if we object to instantaneous connections between objects separated in distance, we have to give up the idea of external reality. Now, submicroscopic objects do not have a concrete reality until they are measured. As a baseball official who was asked to describe his method for umpiring a game put it, "Some is balls and some is strikes, but until I call 'em they ain't nothin'."

It seems that nature has presented us with an image that is an optical illusion. The image itself does not change; it is only our interpretation of it that changes. As with Necker's cube (fig. 5), first we see the cube in one perspective and then in another. The problem is that our eyes are presented with a three-dimensional object drawn on a two-dimensional surface, so our brain does not have enough information to decide between one of two possible interpretations. Perhaps nature, by never letting us see into the box, holds back just enough information to keep us from ever resolving its mysteries. And then again, perhaps there is no mystery. Perhaps we will eventually accept a quantum world just as we have accepted a spherical world.

9

Is Gravity Real?

EINSTEIN'S Special Theory of Relativity revolutionized man's thought about space and time. But revolutionary as the theory was, others had recognized some of its parts. The equations needed to transform from one inertial frame to another, for example, had been anticipated by other scientists. Einstein's genius was to bring all the pieces together and see the whole in a new light.

But Einstein's General Theory of Relativity, his theory of gravitation revealed some ten years later in 1915, is almost exclusively a work of solitary genius. There were no experimental results at great odds with Newton's theory of gravitation, and no one but Einstein was seriously looking for an alternative. At first the theory was accepted as a work of elegant mathematical beauty with limited application, but with the development of precise measuring devices and new developments in astronomy, views of Einstein's General Relativity Theory took on new significance.

As was usual with Einstein, he had begun to worry about Newton's law of gravitation for some very simple reasons. First there was the age-old but unresolved problem of how gravitation acted over the immense expanse of space. Newton had suspected that ether might provide a medium, but Einstein had done away with the ether in Special Relativity.

Another problem had to do with the time it took Newton's gravitational force to act. Its law implies that the gravitational force acts instantaneously over any distance, whereas Special Relativity said that nothing could act instantaneously because all interactions could proceed no faster than the speed of light.

Further, Special Relativity suggested that something was wrong with the form of the law itself. We recall that Newton's gravitational law says that the force between two bodies depends on the distance that separates them and on their masses, but from Special Relativity we know that mass and distance depend on the observer's state of motion; so Newton's law gives different answers for different observers.

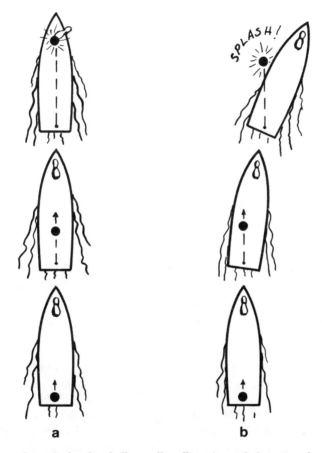

Figs. 1A and B. The bowling ball actually rolls in a straight line. But observers on the ship see it take a curved path, falling off the deck.

And then there was the strange business of Galileo's objects with different masses accelerating toward the earth at the same rate. How is it, Einstein wondered, that objects with such different mass are treated the same by gravity. Other forces do not act that way. If we throw a baseball and a cannonball with the same force, they don't behave in the same way; the baseball nearly disappears from view, and the cannonball drops to the ground in front of the thrower.

Einstein began to realize that gravity acts like what are sometimes called unreal or fictitious forces. To illustrate, let's suppose you are on the deck of a very large ship, and you roll a bowling ball along the length of the deck toward a single bowling pin some distance away (fig. 1A). Since you are a good bowler, you always hit the pin. And then, for no apparent reason, you begin to miss. Each time you see the ball head for the pin and then slowly curve away. It seems as if some invisible force is pulling on your ball, causing it to miss the pin.

But the explanation is very simple: although you don't know it, the ship is slowly turning so that it is no longer an inertial frame of reference, it is no longer moving uniformly in a straight line. What you take for an invisible force is simply the deck of the ship changing its direction beneath the straight-line motion of the bowling ball. If you could watch the ball from a helicopter, you would see it move straight ahead while the ship turned underneath (fig. 1B). You can get rid of the strange force by just changing your point of view, but you can't get rid of a real force by changing your point of view; two magnets tugging on each other do so from anybody's point of view.

It occurred to Einstein that gravity might be something like the bowling ball and the turning ship. His thinking might have gone something like this: Suppose that several objects are floating together in outer space. If we pulled up to them in our spaceship, we might see an old shoe, a hammer, a paper clip, and a large rock all motionless in space with respect to each other.

But suppose another spaceship approached the debris with ever-increasing speed, and then went on past, still accelerating. The people in the speeding spaceship could say, pointing to Special Relativity, that they were at rest and that it was the debris that accelerated past them under the influence of some force. They notice that this force acts just like gravity; the rock, the paper clip, the shoe, and the hammer all "fall" past the spaceship together. In fact, the people in the spaceship say that the force *is* gravity.

Fig. 2. All the car occupants are thrown back together.

They say this because they believe they are at rest, and they feel a force pulling on them in the same direction in which the objects sail by. But we say that is nonsense. What they believe to be gravitational force is simply due to the fact that their spaceship is accelerating; it's the same kind of force that we feel when our bodies are pressed against the back of the seat of an accelerating automobile (fig. 2). We all fall back toward the seat together whether we weigh 80 pounds or 180, just as all objects fall toward the earth with the same acceleration.

Again Einstein took the obvious and turned it into a great principle of nature. He said that if you were in a spaceship with no windows, and you felt a force, there would be no way to tell whether the force was due to the ship's acceleration or simply to the fact that the ship was at rest on the surface of some massive body such as the earth. This principle is called the Principle of Equivalence, and it is a cornerstone of the General Theory of Relativity.

Using this principle we can transform away the force of gravity by moving to a suitable accelerating frame of reference; it's like watching the rotating ship from a helicopter. Standing on the earth's surface we feel the tug of gravity on our body, but if we stepped into an elevator freely falling toward the center of the earth, gravity would disappear. We, and objects with us, would float around inside the elevator just as though we and the objects were in outer space completely free of any gravitational force. Similarly, if an elevator in outer space began to accelerate, we would feel a force; and there would be no way to tell, if our elevator had no windows, whether we were at rest experiencing a gravitational force or whether our elevator was accelerating.

What all this suggests is that the gravitational force, like the force produced by the rotating ship, is no more real than the force we experience in an accelerating automobile. Gravitation must have something to do with the properties of time and space; it is not some independent force acting within the stage of time and space.

Let's return to our free-falling elevator, which we shall assume is very spacious, having room for a billiard table. If we played billiards on this table, nothing would seem strange. Since the table and the balls fall together, the balls continue to roll around on the table as usual. We would observe no violations of Newton's laws of motion or the expanded version of these laws contained in the Special Theory of Relativity. We recall that these laws apply only to inertial—uniformly moving—frames of reference.

But an outside observer would say that this was not the case at all. From his point of view, the elevator is an accelerating frame of reference. How can we reconcile these two points of view?

The answer is related to what Einstein considered to be one of the main defects in his Special Theory of Relativity: it applied only to inertial frames of reference. He believed that a complete theory would include accelerated frames of reference, and further, that the form of the equations would be the same for all observers whether they were in inertial or accelerated frames of reference. As things stood with Special Relativity, the equations had to be altered for accelerated frames.

To put the matter more philosophically, Einstein believed that the laws of nature should be the same for all observers, accelerated or not. As we might expect by now, solving the problem for accelerated frames of reference also provided a new theory of gravitation. Let's see if we can follow the steps leading to this new theory.

First Einstein assumed that the Principle of Equivalence is correct and applies to all frames of reference, both inertial and accelerated, just as in Special Relativity he assumed that the velocity of light is the same for all observers. This means that we can't tell the difference between accelerated frames of reference, producing fictitious forces, and gravity. In assuming this equality between accelerated frames of reference and gravity, Einstein had to stipulate that the equality holds only over small regions of space. This is because gravity is not uniform throughout space but varies from one place to another depending on the distribution of mass in space. That is, there is not one single accelerated frame of reference that can transform gravity away over all space; rather, many different accelerated frames are required, each depending on the local gravitational conditions.

We need to add that since mass and energy are equivalent, from $E = mc^2$, the distribution of mass responsible for the local variations in gravitation includes the distribution of energy in space as well. So from now on when we talk about the distribution of mass in space, we mean to include the distribution of energy.

Let's apply the Principle of Equivalence to the concepts of space and time as we developed them in Special Relativity. There we learned that time runs more slowly for moving clocks and that objects shorten in the direction of motion. Let's suppose we have a merry-go-round and three clocks. One clock is at the center of the merry-go-round, another on the edge of the merry-go-round, and the third sits on the ground. The clocks at the center of the merry-go-round and on the ground tick at the same rate because they do not move relative to each other, but the one on the edge of the merry-go-round runs more slowly because of its motion.

If we stood at the edge of the merry-go-round, we would feel a fictitious force as though the merry-go-round was trying to throw us off. Of course, what is really happening is that the merry-go-round, at the spot where we are standing, is constantly changing direction— just as the ship rotated under the bowling ball—giving us a sense that a force is acting on us. But by the Principle of Equivalence we can replace this fictitious force with gravity. In other words, if we were standing blindfolded on the edge of the merry-go-round, we couldn't tell whether it was rotating or standing still, with the force we felt generated by some massive object near its edge (fig. 3). Now we see how gravity, acceleration, and time are all related through the Principle of Equivalence.

Similarly, let's suppose a ruler is located along the edge of the merry-go-round and another lies on the ground. Because of the merry-go-round's motion, the ruler riding on it will appear shorter to the observer on the ground than the one lying at his feet. Once again we can replace the spinning merry-go-round with a massive object, using the Principle of Equivalence, and conclude that the ruler would also contract in the presence of gravity, which in turn depends on mass and energy.

We saw in Chapter 7 how Einstein collapsed Newton's absolute

Fig. 3. To a blindfolded observer, gravitational and fictitious forces are the same.

space and time into spacetime. With General Relativity, something equally remarkable has happened. In Special Relativity, massive objects and energy moved through spacetime; but in General Relativity, energy, mass, and spacetime are merged to give us spacetime–energy–mass. That is, spacetime and energy-mass are one connected whole. We have a grand fusion of the stage, the actors, and the action. And gravity, which was a force in Newton's world, is now simply a property of spacetime.

Since spacetime is determined by the distribution of mass and energy throughout the universe, we can no longer think of space as being the kind that Euclid discussed in his geometry. There parallel straight lines never meet, and the circumference of a circle is pi times the circle's diameter. But in General Relativity, space is not uniform everywhere; it is "curved" depending on the local distribution of mass and energy. Far away from any mass we have Euclid's uniform space, but near any massive object, be it a marble or the sun, we have curved space; of course, it is far more curved in the vicinity of a massive, dense object like the sun than it is near a marble. We can imagine a thin sheet of rubber stretched over an empty swimming pool. If nothing rests on the sheet, it is flat, like Euclidian space. If we place a marble on the sheet, it depresses slightly, corresponding to a slight curvature of space; but if we place a cannonball on the sheet, it depresses greatly, corresponding to severe space curvature.

How, then, is Einstein's General Theory of Relativity to account for the motion of the earth about the sun? Newton's first law says that a body continues in a straight line unless acted on by some force. In the case of the earth, it is continuously deflected from its straight-line path by the tug of the sun, so that it moves in an elliptical path about the sun.

The phrase *straight line* is the crux of the matter. What does it mean to have a straight line in curved space? Well, in normal Euclidian space, a straight line is the shortest distance between two points. An easy way to trace this path is simply to follow the path of a light beam. In fact, laser light-beams are routinely used today by civil engineers as a means for laying out straight lines.

Let's extend this idea to curved space: the equivalent of a straight line in curved space, a *geodesic*, is the path taken by a beam of light. To return to our rubber sheet, if we rolled a ping-pong ball across the sheet it would move in a straight line unless the sheet were distorted by some object such as a cannonball. Then it would take a curved path. In the first case the geodesic corresponds to our usual notion of straight-line motion in flat space, whereas in the second case the geodesic is curved.

To see what this means, let's return to our freely falling elevator. Suppose one side of our elevator contains a small window through which an outside observer shines a pulse of light. As figure 4A shows, the light enters the window, moving across the falling elevator. The observer outside, who does not know the General Theory of Relativity, believes the light should move in a straight-line horizontal path across the elevator. He will say further that the observer inside the elevator should see the path of the light pulse curve upward, relative to the elevator, as the elevator accelerates downward in its free fall toward the center of the earth.

But by the Principle of Equivalence there is no way for the observer in the elevator to know whether he is falling freely in space or is in

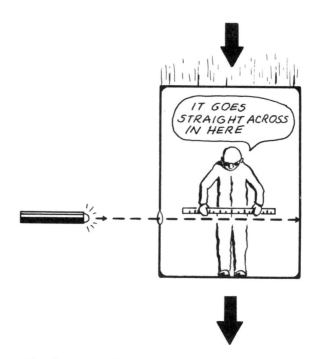

Fig. 4A. The observer in the elevator sees the light move in a straight line.

outer space beyond the influence of any gravitational force. For him the pulse must move in a straight line across the elevator.

But if this is true, the outside observer must see a downward curving path. As figure 4-b shows, much to the outside observer's surprise, this is exactly what he does see. In other words, he must conclude that light takes a curved path rather than a straight path when gravity is present—it moves along a geodesic. Thus in the language of General Relativity, Newton's first law becomes, "An object moves along a geodesic unless some real force like a rocket blast—not a fictitious force—changes its direction of motion." In the framework of General Relativity, the motion of an object caused by the presence of mass is automatically taken care of by the curved nature of spacetime.

For all practical purposes, in our everyday lives spacetime is flat; it is Euclidian. So it is impossible to visualize curved spacetime in any natural way. But we can get some feel for the ideas we've been developing by considering a simple example: suppose two friends and their two small dogs stand at the south end of a football field aligned in a north-south direction. They position themselves so that they and their dogs are exactly 100 feet apart along an east-west line (fig. 5). At some moment all four move at the same speed toward the north end of the field. When they reach the north end, they stop and measure their separation; to no one's surprise, they are still 100 feet apart.

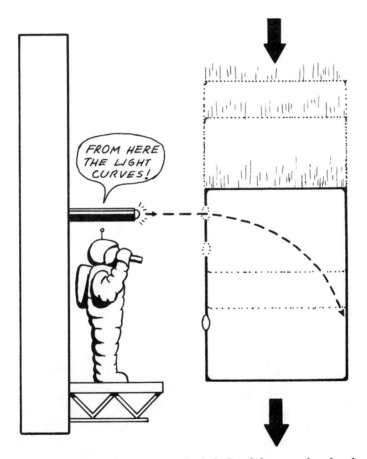

Fig. 4B. The outside observer sees the light bend downward under the force of gravity.

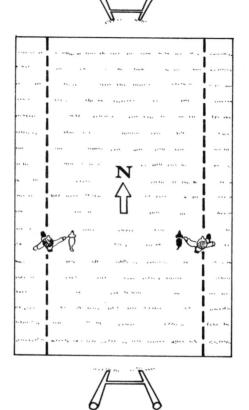

Fig. 5. The marchers are separated by the same distance at both ends of the football field.

Fig. 6. The marchers' paths converge as they approach the North Pole.

But suppose they could continue their northward march, finally coming within sight of the North Pole. Now if they measured their east-west separation they would find it considerably less than 100 feet; in fact, at the pole their paths and their dogs' paths would all join (fig. 6).

Of course, *we* know that their paths approach each other because they are marching along the curved surface of the earth, but to *them* the earth appears flat, so they must account for the closing of their paths in some other way. Their best guess is that some strange force pulls both them and their dogs together as they march northward. They also notice that the force acts equally on them and their dogs, although the dogs are very small.

In much the same way, General Relativity says that the force of gravity is not real but is simply a property of spacetime, the curvature of which depends on the distribution of mass; and objects, unless acted upon by a real force, simply move along geodesics in curved spacetime.

From a mathematical standpoint, the General Theory of Relativity is much more complex than Newton's laws of motion and gravitation. But the theory also resolves many of the problems that plagued Newton's formulation. The problems of a mysterious force acting across space instantaneously and bodies with different masses accelerating at the same rate have disappeared into the curvature of spacetime. And the theory incorporates Einstein's belief that the same equations should apply to both uniform and accelerated frames of reference.

In a way, going from Newton to Einstein is like expanding the words in the vocabulary of a language. In this process we often create a new word to stand for several words. A small child might say, "I saw a funny animal with a long tail swinging through the trees." When he is older he expresses the same thought with, "I saw a monkey swinging through the trees"—a saving of five words. Of course, to realize this saving he had to learn a new word. Similarly, the vocabulary of mathematics needed to express the General Theory of Relativity contains many symbols, each standing for a complex idea. In the appropriate mathematical language, the symbols representing the General Theory occupy less than the half page required by Newton's laws of motion and gravitation, but the ideas expressed by these symbols go well beyond those contained in Newton's symbols. Anyone who has taken the time to learn the mathematics of the General Theory quite easily understands the beauty, simplicity, and appeal of its equations.

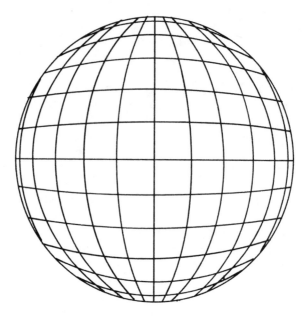

Fig. 7. In global symmetries the lines of latitude and longitude maintain their relative positions as the sphere rotates.

They represent, even more than Newton's equations, the ideals of Ockham's razor and Greek symmetry. All observers, whether moving uniformly or with acceleration, have an equal footing; and the theory puts space, time, gravity, acceleration, energy, and mass into one package.

In Chapter 5 we saw how Maxwell's electromagnetic equations incorporate the idea that the speed of light is the same for all observers. Einstein's General Theory of Relativity also incorporates an important concept that appears to be the key to developing our understanding of all the forces of nature. This concept was noticed shortly after Einstein published his theory, but it was not developed in a particularly fruitful way at the time. The concept is highly mathematical and abstract, so we can only suggest what it involves in the following analogy:

In the Special Theory of Relativity, we found that the laws of nature are the same for all observers in inertial frames of reference. Conversely, we could say that all observers in inertial frames of refer-

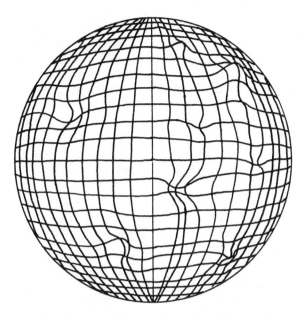

Fig. 8. In local symmetries the lines of latitude and longitude are distorted at various locations on the sphere.

ence would discover the same laws of nature. This suggests a kind of global character of the laws of nature for observers in inertial frames. This kind of uniformity or symmetry of the laws of nature is in fact called *global symmetry.*

We can symbolize this global symmetry by picturing a globe of the earth with its grid of north-south lines of longitude and east-west lines of latitude. If we rotate the globe along an axis running through the north and south poles, the grid stays intact; it is not distorted in any way. We can think of this distortionless rotation as being similar to the equations of Special Relativity retaining their form as we move from one inertial system to another (fig. 7).

Now let's consider General Relativity in the same vein. Here we wish to expand the idea of the equations maintaining their same form to observers in accelerated frames of reference—in spaceships moving at different accelerations, for example. We can no longer transform one reference frame to another that holds for all points in space, for we no longer have global symmetry. We have to consider each point on a local basis. That is, we require a kind of local symmetry where each point in space can be transformed independently of any other point and still maintain the laws of nature in the same form. This local symmetry requirement is much more stringent than a global symmetry, but the local symmetry requirement contains the seeds of gravitation.

Let's imagine that our globe is made from a balloon. Our local symmetry requirement amounts to pushing and pulling the different points on the balloon's surface in different directions, but always keeping each point at the same distance from the balloon's center so that it maintains its shape. That is, the overall spherical symmetry of the balloon is retained (fig. 8). Because the balloon is stretched differently here and there, tensions develop between different parts of the balloon.

Now we see that our requirement for local symmetry has introduced a system of forces in the balloon's surface that weren't there before. If we wished to remove those forces we would need to introduce a new set of forces that would exactly counteract the forces in the balloon. In our crude analogy, those counteracting forces are the gravitational forces. In other words, introducing the force of gravitation allows the laws of nature to remain the same in any frame of reference, and so to remove the tensions in the balloon. Putting all this together we have the General Theory of Relativity.

If we imagine ourselves in a spaceship in outer space, we can consider a specific example of local symmetry. Freely moving in outer space, we would find all the laws of nature intact. Furthermore, another traveler in a spaceship moving freely and parallel to ours—say 10 kilometers away—would conclude that the laws of nature he observes are identical to the ones we observe in our ship. This is an example of *global* symmetry.

But suppose we steer our ship into a circular path. Now we feel a force pushing us against the side of the ship. Of course we know that what is really happening is that, by Newton's first law, our bodies tend to continue in a straight line, but this tendency is being constantly frustrated by the circular motion of the space ship, creating a fictitious force.

Suppose we fall asleep and waken later to find that the force pushing us against the side of the ship is gone. Our first thought is that the ship has resumed its straight-line motion. But inspection of the navigation control panel shows that the ship is still taking a circular path. We glance out the nearest window and resolve the mystery: Our spaceship is orbiting the earth. The fictitious force caused by our circular motion has been exactly balanced by the earth's gravity. We again find all the laws of motion intact, just as we had found them in outer space. In other words, orbiting the earth in a circular path is just like straight-line motion in outer space, and the thing that makes this true is gravitation. Gravitation is essential if we are to have local symmetry—if we are to have the same laws for observers moving in any manner whatever.

These two symmetries—global and local symmetries—are usually called *gauge* symmetries. Although the word *gauge* does not give much of a hint of its meaning as used here, it originally sprang from the idea that different measuring devices, such as rulers, should give the same result whether the measurements are made in inches, centimeters, or whatever. That is, one's height does not change because he measures it in centimeters instead of inches. In this sense, gauge symmetries incorporate a related idea that the laws of nature are the same for all observers.

It's natural to wonder whether the other forces of nature, such as the electromagnetic force, are not also fictitious, simply being some property of spacetime. Until the end of his life, Einstein sought to bring gravitational and electromagnetic forces together into one unified curved spacetime theory—his Unified Field Theory—but the goal, like a rainbow, remained forever beyond his reach. That is still true today. This is not to say that photons of light, having energy and therefore an equivalent mass, are not subject to General Relativity, but so far, gravity occupies the central position in the idea that all laws of nature should be the same for all observers no matter what their motion.

The unified theory that Einstein sought is also complicated by the fact that we now know there are two other forces to account for; these were discovered in the attempt to understand atoms and other elementary particles. In Chapter 12 we shall discuss the search to bring all of nature's four forces together into one unified whole guided by the principle of gauge symmetry. That will require us to return once more to the submicroscopic world. But before we do that, we shall see in the next chapter what General Relativity has revealed to us, not about the submicroscopic world, but about the nature of the entire universe.

10

A Most Singular Affair

LIKE LEONARDO DA VINCI'S *Mona Lisa* and Beethoven's *Ninth Symphony*, Einstein's General Theory of Relativity is one of the world's masterworks. As with any great artistic triumph, it is at once simple and profound, of enduring interest, and created with abandon in an environment of the severest discipline. Einstein could no more have created his theory without deeply studying nature than Michelangelo could have sculpted his *David* without a master builder's feel for marble.

Even if General Relativity had not so profoundly advanced our knowledge of the universe, it would still be considered a magnificent structure because it insisted that there are no privileged positions in the universe. It says that democracy reigns supreme in the underlying architecture of the cosmos, that all corners of the universe are governed in the same fashion. This principle of universal relativity, even if Einstein had developed it wrongly, is one of the most powerful inventions of man's mind. It has led us, and continues to lead us, to an ever deeper understanding of the workings of the universe.

When Copernicus dethroned the earth from the center of the solar system, he started a movement that Einstein firmly embraced and expanded as he set out to apply his General Theory of Relativity to the universe. He said not only that we are not the center of the solar system, but that we occupy a position in the universe that is very ordinary. He further stated that one part of the universe is much like any other part. So not only are the laws the same for all observers throughout the universe, but the very universe itself, as viewed on the large scale, is the same throughout. If we were lost in the universe, it would do no good to look around for a familiar landmark to get our bearings, for in the universe Boston and Tokyo are much the same.

Einstein called his belief in the uniformity of the universe his Cosmological Principle. With this principle and General Relativity, he made it possible, for the first time, for science to provide some insight to the character of the universe. Previously the subject had been purely within the domain of philosophers and theologians.

Einstein's paper concerning the nature of the universe appeared about a year after his paper on General Relativity. As we have seen, General Relativity reveals the deep connection between matter and spacetime. As a starting point, Einstein had to assume something about the distribution of matter in spacetime, which then dictates the nature of the curvature of space. Then, and today, it appears that the universe is, on the average, "smooth," although obviously we have concentrations of matter here and there in the form of stars, galaxies, and so on. In any case, anywhere we look, the universe seems to be the same. It is not possible to see the entire universe, however; so there may be parts of it, invisible to us, that are not uniform. But Einstein's Cosmological Principle assumed that the universe was smooth throughout, and proceeded from there.

The observations of the universe also seemed to suggest one other fact: The universe was static, not dynamic. The stars, as far as anyone could tell, maintained their positions in the heavens. The universe as a whole was neither expanding nor contracting, and thus, apparently, had no beginning or end. Aside from this observational evidence, the notion that the universe is static and eternal was embedded in most of the world's philosophies of the time and embraced by many religions—"from everlasting to everlasting."

We can imagine Einstein's great shock, then, when he discovered that his Cosmological Principle, coupled with General Relativity, demanded a dynamic universe; the universe was either expanding or contracting. Einstein found this result so unacceptable that he changed his theory so that it would predict a static universe, but probably even then he was not entirely comfortable with this doctoring of his equations. As we shall see, his discomfort was justified because if he had "stuck to his guns" he would have made one of the most phenomenal predictions of all time—the dynamic universe.

To the general public, the most curious aspect of Einstein's universe was that it was not infinite but neither was it bounded. This was because, with the distribution of matter that Einstein had assumed, the universe curved back on itself so that if a traveler set out on a journey away from the earth, he would eventually find himself back at home without ever encountering an edge to the universe.

In our ordinary flat, Euclidian space, the closest analogy is the surface of a sphere such as our earth; the surface area is finite, and yet it has no boundaries. It is interesting that Giordano Bruno, who was burned at the stake for his heretical views on the universe, prophetically said, "We can say with certainty that the universe is all center, or that the center of the universe is everywhere and the circumference is nowhere."

In the years between 1917 and 1929, a number of theorists explored Einstein's General Theory of Relativity and discovered some models that had not occurred to him. In particular, a Russian mathematician, Alexander Friedmann, whose primary interest was weather, discovered a solution to the equations Einstein had originally proposed—not his doctored equations. In this solution, still assuming the Cosmological Principle, the universe was either expanding or collapsing; which happened depended on the density of the average mass distribution throughout the universe. If the density was above a certain level, the universe would eventually collapse; below a certain level, it would expand forever.

In these dynamic models it was not that matter is expanding or contracting about some location in Newton's great, infinite stage of space and time, but rather that space itself is either expanding or

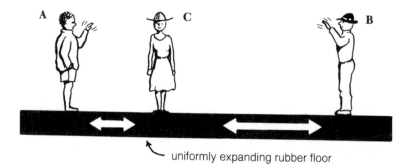

Fig. 1. The greater the distance between objects, the greater the speed with which they move apart. B moves away from C twice as fast as A.

contracting, and matter embedded in this space separates or closes on itself as the space expands or contracts. It is as if we are standing on a rubber floor expanding or contracting under our feet (fig. 1). If the floor expands, we move away from our neighbors even though we are not walking. And the farther away a neighbor is, the faster he recedes from us: A neighbor 20 feet away recedes twice as fast as one 10 feet away. This is because the floor is everywhere expanding, so there is twice as much floor to expand between us and a neighbor who is initially 20 feet away as there is between us and another who is only 10 feet away.

In 1929, some twelve years after Einstein had modified his theory, a former lawyer, Edwin Hubble, announced that the universe was expanding. When Einstein learned of Hubble's discovery, he told George Gamow—whom we shall meet again and who was a onetime assistant to Alexander Friedmann—that changing his theory had been "the biggest blunder of my life."

Hubble, born in Missouri and educated as a lawyer at Oxford, had been an outstanding student and athlete in college. At one time he fought an exhibition match with the world light-heavyweight champion and was urged by many to pursue boxing. But his interests were in academic subjects, and he attended Oxford University as a Rhodes scholar. In 1913 he returned to Louisville, Kentucky, to practice law, but gave it up after a few months to study astronomy. In 1919, after being wounded in World War I, he went to Mount Wilson Observatory in California, where the new 100-inch telescope was installed. There, over the next ten years, he discovered that the universe was expanding.

From the beginning, Hubble had been interested in the strange, cloudlike stellar objects we now call *spiral galaxies*. With the 100-inch telescope, he could see that each cloud was actually thousands of stars spiraling in cosmic swirls around a bright inner core. Were these galaxies a part of our own local system of stars—our own galaxy—or were they whole systems of stars at distances never before imagined? Using a combination of techniques, made more powerful by the 100-inch telescope, Hubble showed that the galaxies were not a part of our own galaxy, but more amazing, the farther away the galaxy was, the greater its speed from us.

One of the techniques Hubble used depends on the characteristic "fingerprints" that atoms have. We recall that particular atoms emit radiation at particular frequencies; so their presence in distant stars can be identified. If a star is moving away from an observer, the

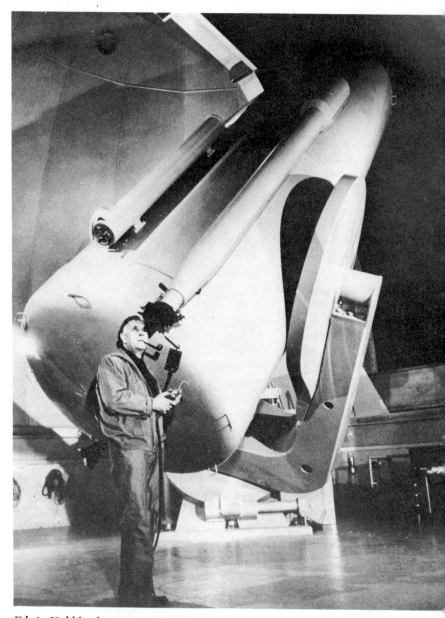

Edwin Hubble observing with the 48-inch Schmidt telescope at Palomar—
the Hale Observatories.

characteristic frequencies move to lower values, just as the whistle of a departing train is lower in frequency than the same whistle heard when the train is standing still. In this way Hubble concluded that the distant galaxies are moving away from us.

A new picture of the universe was emerging. It consisted of galaxies—nobody knew how many—all fleeing from each other. The universe was expanding, but what had it expanded from? And why? A model of an expanding universe, if run backward in time—like running a movie backwards—shows a universe, with all its matter, shrinking to a single point. But at the time, no one took that possibility seriously.

A star is somewhat like a miniature version of the universe: It consists of thousands and billions of atoms and other elementary particles all interacting with each other under the influence of gravity. The gravitational force acts to pull all the particles together into a single point—like the beginning of the shrinking-universe model run backwards. Another force—and here our parallel with the universe ends—supplied by the nuclear furnace at the center of the star pushes the particles of the star outward. These two opposing forces are balanced so that a star does not appreciably expand or contract. But what happens when the nuclear furnace burns out and there is nothing to oppose the inward force of gravitation?

The question was answered in 1939 by Robert Oppenheimer, the American physicist who headed the project leading to the first nuclear explosion in the New Mexico desert. Oppenheimer showed that, after the nuclear furnace died down, the star would collapse into a point under its own gravity. But no one took that prediction seriously either. Even Einstein wrote a paper later that same year saying such collapsed objects could not exist. And there the controversy stood until the early 1960s.

Since Galileo's time the optical telescope had been astronomers' most useful tool, but in the 1950s a new kind of telescope, the radio telescope, appeared. Where the optical telescope concentrated the light from distant objects in the sky, the radio telescope did the same for distant objects emitting radio waves—radio stars. These stars, in contrast to normal stars, seemed to be diffuse, not concentrated into a point. But a few were pointlike, and the radio astronomers called them "quasi-stellar radio sources," or *quasars*.

After a dozen or so quasars had been identified, it was natural to wonder, because of their pointlike appearance, if quasars had any connection with ordinary stars. So astronomers aimed their optical

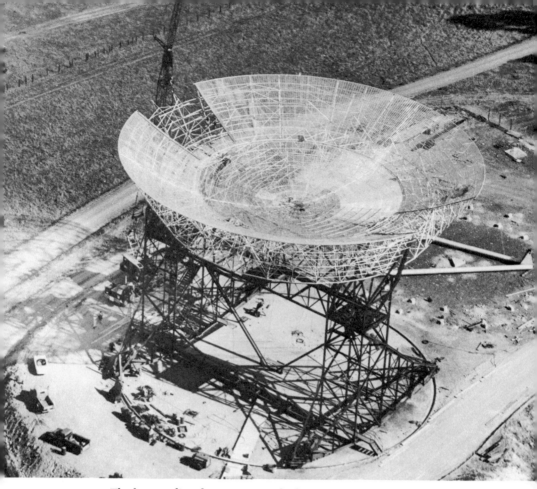

The huge radio-telescope at Stanford University

telescopes in the directions of some of the quasars. In almost all cases, a point of faint light appeared as though a new star had been found. But there was one startling difference: For these stars the fingerprint radiation emissions were shifted to unheard-of lower frequencies, indicating that the quasars were moving away from us at extremely high speed, and therefore were also at unbelievable distances. This meant that they might have been larger than ordinary stars, but only appeared pointlike because of their extreme distance.

Over the years, more quasars were discovered, some moving away at almost the speed of light. This meant that astronomers were beginning to see to the very edge of the observable universe—observable because an object moving at the speed of light would never be seen because its radiation would never reach us.

There was another thing. Ordinary stars at such a distance would not be visible with even the most powerful telescopes. The fact that telescopes could detect such objects at all at such great distances meant that quasars could not be ordinary stars. Quasars, whatever they are, are extremely bright.

Furthermore, they have to be small compared to ordinary galaxies because they fluctuate in brightness. If a quasar were extremely large, it could not "organize itself" to fluctuate as one whole unit. The problem is something like using a powerful megaphone to command a long column of troops to march; the troops near the megaphone hear the command before the troops far away, so the whole column cannot step forward together (fig. 2). In the same sense, a quasar must be compact if its various parts are to fluctuate in brightness together. Whatever mechanism causes the quasar to fluctuate cannot act in near-unison over large distances; according to the theory of Special Relativity, the finite velocity of light—and thus of any coordinating mechanism—prohibits this.

These compactness arguments indicate that if an ordinary galaxy were the size of a covered football stadium like the Astrodome, then the quasar would be about the size of a pea, but it radiates as much energy as a thousand galaxies lumped together! It is clear that whatever the nature of quasars, they must be compact and massive, and therefore generate very strong gravitational forces.

Here was a problem for General Relativity, and with it a resurrection of the ideas Oppenheimer had developed in his paper on collapsed stars. His 1939 paper began, "When all thermonuclear sources of energy are exhausted, a sufficiently heavy star will collapse

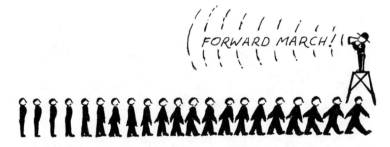

Fig. 2. Not all of the soldiers hear the command at the same time, so they cannot move as one whole unit.

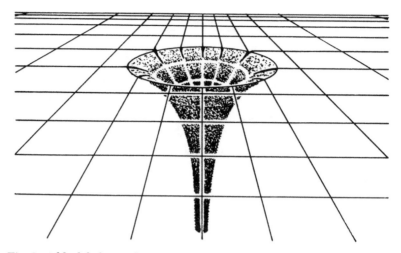

Fig. 3. A black hole is a distortion in spacetime into which everything within its reach is swept.

. . ." and its ". . . contraction will continue indefinitely. . . ." This means that as the star collapses, the density increases so that near the surface the force of gravity becomes so strong that nothing can escape—not even light. Or in terms of General Relativity, spacetime becomes so curved in the neighborhood of the collapsed star that nothing can escape. Furthermore, any matter or radiation approaching this "knot" in spacetime is sucked in, never to be seen again. Today we call these knots in spacetime *black holes* (fig. 3).

But what can a black hole have to do with a quasar? Quasars generate enormous amounts of energy, whereas black holes gobble up everything within reach. Imagine a galaxy whose center contains a massive black hole—perhaps a billion or so stars like our sun collapsed into one black hole. The enormous gravitational force created by this black hole would suck up any matter in its vicinity. As this matter is torn apart by the gravitational forces, some of it is converted into energy that produces all manner of radiation—radio waves, light waves, X rays, and so on.

Calculations show that if something like a thousand sunlike stars were swept into such a black hole every year, enough radiation would be generated to account for the radiation coming from a quasar. But to be fair, we must say that this is only the most accepted theory. No one knows with certainty why quasars are so small and generate so much energy.

When we look at a quasar, we are looking into the past. The most distant quasars seem to be about 15 billion light-years away. A light-year is the distance traveled by a light signal in one year—an enormous distance when we consider that light travels 186,000 miles in one second. So when the light from a quasar 15 billion light years away enters a telescope, it means that the light started its journey 15 billion years ago. Or what amounts to the same thing, we are looking at the universe the way it looked 15 billion years ago. Of course, in a similar way, nearer stars, galaxies, and quasars allow us to see what the universe was like in more recent times.

If we look back much beyond 15 billion years into the past, we see fewer and fewer quasars. This suggests that we are looking at an early stage of the universe when quasars were first forming. In fact, if we look at the present expansion rate of the universe, it suggests that the universe appeared about 15 billion years ago. We get this number simply by noting that if we reverse the known expansion rate, the galaxies would all come together in about 15 billion years.

This brings us back to the black-hole problem. As we go further back in time, the universe gets smaller and smaller, and denser and denser, until it disappears into a point. At least this is what we must believe if General Relativity works at such tiny distances—but we do not believe it.

Physicists and mathematicians say an equation is singular if it gives a result that doesn't seem to make sense. Suppose, for example, that we wish to divide a pie equally among four friends. That's easy; we just give each friend a quarter of the pie. We arrive at this figure by dividing the number 1 by the number 4. But suppose we propose dividing the pie among zero people. That obviously doesn't make any sense, and the mathematics signals us that it doesn't. If we divide one by zero, we get infinity.

What can we make of this answer? Does it mean that no people can eat an infinity of pie? How can zero people eat any pie at all? Of course, what has happened is that we've tried to apply our formula for dividing pie to a situation in which it doesn't work. That's what happens to Einstein's General Relativity equations when we try to apply them to a point. They become singular.

Is there a way out? Most physicists think so, but no one knows the path yet. You will remember that quantum mechanics prescribes nature's laws in the microworld, whereas General Relativity comes into play when we are dealing with massive, very dense bodies. The early universe is both—it is microscopic and massive. And it is this convergence of the microscopic and macroscopic worlds at the beginning of the universe that has started astronomers and physicists talking seriously to one another. What is needed is some kind of marriage between quantum mechanics and General Relativity—as Maxwell merged electricity and magnetism, and Einstein merged space, time, and matter—if we are to understand the emergence of the universe.

We can see, perhaps, in barest outline, what is involved. Einstein's equations, like Newton's, depict the universe as being clocklike— the motion of a particle, whether calculated by Newton's equations or Einstein's, has a completely predictable path. In Einstein's case, this path is determined by the curvature of space, which in turn depends on the distribution and movement of mass at each point in space.

But now a predicament arises. Quantum mechanics says that, on the very small scale, it is meaningless to talk about the location and motion of matter at the same time. If this is true, how are we to specify the distribution of mass at each point in spacetime in order to calculate the path of a particle?

No one knows the answer. We are faced with the kind of paradox that faced the people who believed the earth was flat, yet could not imagine how it could either be infinite or have an edge. As we have 'seen before, out of such confusion and paradox a new view of the universe often emerges. This is an exciting time for scientists. Many believe an answer will be found before the century's end.

We shall consider this subject further in the final chapter, but for now we must add one more point. The singularities in the equations of physics, as we have said before, are a flashing red light that indicates something is wrong. And the problems are very much like dividing by zero. The problems in General Relativity arise from trying to deal with a universe that is zero size. But here quantum mechanics may come to the rescue. Quantum mechanics suggests that there may be no such thing in nature as a point in spacetime—that spacetime is always smeared out, occupying some minimum region. If this is true, it could possibly get rid of the singularities that plague many of the equations of modern physics.

One of the curiosities of this minimum smeared-out volume of spacetime is that it is apparently very much smaller than the atom or even the nucleus of an atom. How can this be, if the building blocks of the universe are atoms? We'll take up this question now.

11

The Particle Zoo

WE LEARNED in Chapter 6 how Ernest Rutherford's probing of atoms with alpha particles made him give up his one-time concept of the atom as ". . . a nice, hard fellow, red or grey in color according to taste." In his revised concept, the atom was a heavy, positively charged nucleus surrounded by a swarm of just enough negatively charged electrons to balance the positive charge of the nucleus.

The simplest and lightest of all atoms, the hydrogen atom, consists of one electron that exactly balances the positive charge of the nucleus (fig. 1). The nucleus of the hydrogen atom is called a *proton*. At first it seemed that all other, heavier atoms were simply built from protons and electrons, the number of protons making up the nucleus being equaled in number by the swarming electrons, so that the net electrical charge was zero.

But it was soon clear that something was wrong. The nucleus of the helium atom has a mass as though it consists of four protons, but it has only two electrons. The first suggestion was that the nucleus contained two electrons which, along with the two circling electrons, produced a net charge of zero. But this idea presented some problems in terms of the growing theoretical understanding of the atom.

A better idea seemed to be that there was an as-yet undiscovered particle whose mass equaled or nearly equaled the mass of the proton but whose charge was zero. In this model, the nucleus of the helium atom consisted of two protons and two "neutral protons." In 1932, James Chadwick, working in Rutherford's laboratory and using alpha particles as probes as Rutherford had done, discovered the neutral proton—the *neutron*. It now seemed that all the universe was built from electrons, protons, and neutrons.

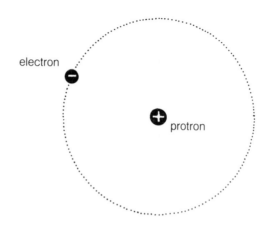

Fig. 1. The proton is the nucleus of the hydrogen atom.

We say seemed because there was a curious result obtained earlier, in 1928, by physicist Paul Dirac. Dirac, perhaps the greatest English theoretical physicist of this century, did what all great theoretical physicists have done: He merged two theories—Special Relativity and quantum mechanics—to produce his *Dirac equation*. The most curious offspring of this marriage was the prediction of a new particle that seemed something like an electron except that it had a positive charge and it was not made from the ordinary matter of the universe. If an ordinary electron and the new particle came together, they disappeared in a flash of energy, their masses being converted into energy according to $E = mc^2$ (fig. 2).

This result once again revolutionized the physicists' conception of the universe. Here was a case where one of the building blocks of the universe, the electron, could vanish. And further, Dirac's equation indicated that, with enough concentration of energy, an electron–new-particle pair could be created. As Werner Heisenberg, one of the inventors of quantum mechanics, said, ". . . up to that time [Dirac's equation] I think every physicist had thought of elementary particles along the lines of the philosophy of Democritus, namely . . . elementary particles as unchangeable units which are . . . always the same thing. After Dirac's discovery everything looked different."

In 1932, the same year Chadwick discovered the neutron, an American physicist, Carl Anderson, spotted a curious track left by an elementary particle on a photographic plate. He was studying the strange rays and particles coming from outer space—cosmic rays—when he noticed the particle track that behaved exactly like an electron except that it curved in the opposite direction in a magnetic field. Anderson named the new particle the *positron*, and two years later received the Nobel Prize in physics for his work. The positron was the particle, formed from the peculiar matter now called antimatter, predicted by Dirac.

But there was more to come in the decade of the 1930s. In earlier studies of radioactive atoms, it had been discovered that the electrons ejected from the nucleus of the atom didn't have as much energy as they should have had. Either one of the strongholds of physics—that energy is neither created nor destroyed—had to be abandoned, or some unseen particle was carrying off part of the energy. This particle, if it existed, was strange indeed. It had no mass—or so little that it could not be detected—and it traveled with the speed of light. The particle was dubbed the *neutrino*—"little neutral one" in Italian—by the Italian physicist Enrico Fermi. The neutrino was finally discovered in 1956, in a nuclear power plant. Although it was found late, few doubted its existence because of the overwhelming belief in the indestructibility of energy.

Now, if the nucleus of an atom consists of protons and neutrons, where do the electrons and the neutrinos come from? That was a question that bothered Fermi. Although he never answered it satisfactorily, theory suggests, as we shall see later, that they are born out

Fig. 2. **When an ordinary electron and the new particle come together, they disappear in a flash of light energy.**

Enrico Fermi

of the nucleus rather than having been there all along. In any case, Fermi was convinced that gravitational and electromagnetic forces were not enough to explain the production of electrons and neutrinos by the nucleus. He proposed that a new force, weaker than the electromagnetic force but stronger than the gravitational force, was needed.

As we have seen, physicists in the years and centuries before

Fermi had been busy combining apparently unrelated forces into unified forces, and now Fermi was saying that a new force was needed. His ideas were guided by the theory of the atom, which says that atoms emit radiation when an electron jumps to a lower orbit, in the form of photons of light. Here we have a case of the energy lost by the atom being turned into something that didn't exist before, the photon. In much the same way, Fermi reasoned that the electrons and neutrinos coming from the atomic nucleus simply represent the fact that some of the energy of the atomic nucleus is being transformed to electrons and neutrinos. It is not a case of a rabbit hidden away in the magician's hat emerging ears first. Rather it is a case of the rabbit being created, from the tips of its ears to its puff of a tail, from some source of energy within the hat, as it appears over the brim.

The new force proposed by Fermi, today called the weak force, is not like the forces of electromagnetism and gravity. These forces extend indefinitely over space, whereas the weak force is very short range, acting only inside the atomic nucleus. Furthermore, it is not an attractive or repulsive force, but a force that brings about transformations. For example, a typical lone neutron, after about fifteen minutes, transforms itself into an electron—a proton and a neutrino—under the influence of the weak force (fig. 3).

Fermi speculated that some new particle—or perhaps particles— was associated with the weak force in the same sense that photons of light go hand in hand with the electromagnetic forces, but he was not able to make any specific predictions. In any case, at least two more particles seemed to be required: the neutrino and the particle

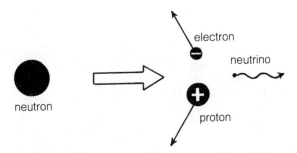

Fig. 3. After about fifteen minutes a neutron transforms into a proton, an electron, and a neutrino.

or particles associated with the new weak force. We shall have more to say about this later.

The last particle that was predicted, and incorrectly thought to be found, in the 1930s developed from a very puzzling aspect of the nucleus of the atom: If the average nucleus consists of neutrons and protons packed together, what force keeps the neutrons and protons together and stops the positively charged protons from flying apart under their mutual electrical repulsion? As we saw earlier, a very small bit of electrical imbalance is enough to fling a battleship into orbit. Whatever holds the nucleus together must be even stronger than the electromagnetic force, and like the electromagnetic force with its photons—and most likely the weak force as conjectured by Fermi—there should be a new particle associated with it.

Before we explore the answer to this puzzle, we need to review some things we already know and see how they relate to the structure and behavior of the atom. As we know, quantum mechanics says it's impossible to measure, or even define, the position and motion of an elementary particle at the same time. This principle is usually called the Heisenberg Uncertainty Principle after Werner Heisenberg, who first pointed it out. Another form of the uncertainty principle says that it is not possible to know simultaneously the time and the amount of energy associated with some event. That is, if we want to know how much energy is involved in the event, we must study it over a period of time; if we study it only momentarily, we are uncertain as to how much energy was involved. This uncertainty has an important implication for the idea that energy is always conserved—that energy cannot be either created or destroyed—when applied to elementary particles like photons and electrons.

Maxwell's electromagnetic equations tell us how to calculate the forces between electrons. We remember that Maxwell was influenced by Faraday's concept of electrical and magnetic lines of force in the development of his equations. Here we imagine that one electron "feels" the other electron via the lines of force produced by the other electron, and vice versa. Maxwell believed that the lines of force were supported by the elusive ether, which Einstein banned. What then is responsible for the electromagnetic force?

Amazingly enough, the energy-time uncertainty principle supplies the answer. As we know, an atom can emit a photon of energy when one of its electrons jumps to an inner orbit. Can an electron standing alone in space emit a photon? The energy-time uncertainty principle

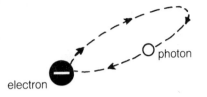

Fig. 4. A photon can exist momentarily from energy borrowed from an electron.

says that it can, as long as the emitted photon returns to its parent electron after a very short time. It's a little like a soldier being told by his commanding officer that he can't leave his post, but then he notices that his commanding officer isn't always watching. Since the officer won't know the soldier is gone, if the soldier is quick enough and doesn't stay away too long, he can violate the order.

In a similar way, an electron can "borrow" enough energy momentarily to emit a photon if the photon is not gone too long (fig. 4). In other words, from the time-energy uncertainty principle, we know that it takes time to know precisely how much energy is carried off by the photon; so if the photon returns "home" very quickly, nature will never notice that a photon existed briefly. This means that if the time is short enough, the principle of the conservation of energy can be violated. Or if we think of the momentary photon from a measurement point of view, we can say that since we can know how much energy is involved only imprecisely in a short measurement of time, we can't insist on the conservation of energy any more than we can measure it. Although this behavior seems bizarre, a number of definitive experiments show that electrons are continually surrounded by not just one, but by a swarm of photons on short trips away from home.

Suppose now that two electrons approach each other with their swarms of photons. As the electrons come closer together, one or more photons may venture far enough from home to impact and be absorbed by the other electron. We can think of the photons as being like a shower of snowballs flying back and forth between the two electrons (fig. 5). And like the opponents in a snowball fight, the electrons retreat from each other under the assault of the photons. Maxwell's mysterious electromagnetic force turns out to be a mutual bombardment of photons. Today these are called *exchange* forces.

From left to right: Niels Bohr, Hideki Yukawa, Mrs. Yukawa, and J. Robert Oppenheimer.

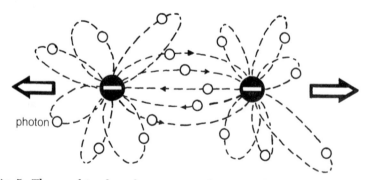

photon

Fig. 5. The repulsive force between two electrons is like two combatants retreating from each other under a shower of snowballs.

In 1935 a young Japanese physicist, Hideki Yukawa, proposed a theory to explain the force that holds an atom's nucleus together. His reasoning was similar to some ideas developed earlier by Dirac and Fermi in their studies of the interactions between photons and electrons. Just as an electron can momentarily produce a photon, Yukawa reasoned, a proton (or a neutron) could also momentarily produce a particle. And if two protons approach each other, they may exchange particles. In this case, however, the particle exchange holds the particles together like two people throwing a beach ball back and forth. The players must always stand within throwing range of each other for the game to continue (fig. 6).

Yukawa's calculations predicted that the mass of this particle— which Yukawa called a *meson*—should be about three hundred times the mass of the electron, and that its associated force, now called the strong force, would be enough to hold the nucleus together. As we might expect, the strong force is another exchange force.

It appeared that just such a particle was found in cosmic rays in 1936 by Carl Anderson, who had discovered the positron. But although Anderson's particle was an unknown particle something like a fat electron and now called the *muon*, its mass was wrong; and Yukawa's predicted particle, the *pion*, was finally found in 1946 in cosmic ray showers.

Fig. 6. The strong force is something like two people held together by a beach ball they are tossing back and forth.

By the end of the 1930s, nature's basic forces had increased from two to four: gravitational, electromagnetic, weak, and strong forces. And besides the electron and proton, there were now the neutron, the neutrino, the muon, and the particles predicted by Fermi and Yukawa for the weak and strong forces. But this was just the beginning. The particle zoo had only begun to form.

As we have seen, most of the new particles were discovered in cosmic ray showers. Such showers are produced by particles from outer space, mostly protons, smashing into the atoms and molecules of the atmosphere and breaking them down into smaller, subatomic particles like the *pion*.

In 1947 new and unusual particles, called V *particles* because they left V-shaped tracks in cosmic ray photos, were discovered. The V particles seemed to be created under the influence of the strong force, but disappeared—or decayed, as particle physicists say—under the influence of the weak force. Because of this strange behavior, they came to be called *strange* particles.

As early as the late 1920s, it was suggested that machines could be built to smash atoms and other particles together to see what they were made of, just as the particles in cosmic rays crashed into the atmosphere and revealed new particles. These machines, popularly called atom smashers are now common. By the early 1960s more than a hundred new subatomic particles had been revealed by atom smashers or found in cosmic rays. This proliferation provided a situation similar to the one that Mendeleyev faced when he tried to find some kind of pattern in the dozens of elements that were known in his time. Later developments, of course, showed that all elements could be built from collections of protons, neutrons, and electrons, thus reducing over a hundred elements to different patterns of just three particles.

But with the flurry of new particles in the 1960s—the positron, the muon, the pion, the neutrino, the V particles, and dozens of other subatomic particles—it seemed, for the time being at least, that the universe could not be understood in terms of a few basic building blocks. The question now was: Are there just a few basic particles that could be combined to explain the subatomic particle zoo?

One of the scientists thinking about this problem was Murray Gell-Mann, a physicist at the California Institute of Technology. As Mendeleyev had seen a pattern for the elements, so Gell-Mann perceived a pattern in the particle zoo. He called this pattern the *eight-fold way* after certain Buddhist teachings that proposed eight guideposts to life. The pattern of eight seemed appropriate because eight related particles, all subject to the strong force, could be laid out in a particular way, much as Mendeleyev had laid out his table. And just as Mendeleyev's pattern seemed incomplete, leading him to predict new elements, so Gell-Mann, from his pattern, predicted the *omega-minus* particle, which was discovered in 1964.

In 1963 Gell-Mann and another American, George Zweig, independently discovered a mathematical scheme for classifying the atomic and subatomic particles that seemed to require variations on three components. These components were not identified with a new set of elementary particles, but were simply mathematical elements in their theory, out of which they could construct most of the atomic and subatomic particles known at the time. Gell-Mann called the elements *quarks* because, he said, he liked the sound of the word, which was from an obscure line in James Joyce's book *Finnegan's Wake:* "Three Quarks for Muster Mark." And three quarks were just what Gell-Mann needed to build protons, neutrons, strange particles, and most of the other particles known at the time.

According to Gell-Mann, quarks came in three varieties called up, down, and strange; and they had a charge of either plus two-thirds of the electron's charge or minus one-third of its charge. The proton was made from two up quarks and one down quark, and the neutron consisted of two down quarks and one up quark. Mesons

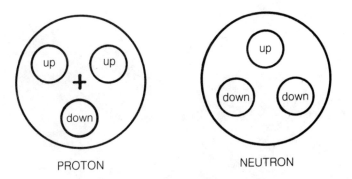

PROTON   NEUTRON

Fig. 7. A proton is made from two up and one down quarks, and a neutron is made from two down and one up quarks.

were made from a quark and another quark made out of antimatter called an *antiquark*. And, of course, the strange quarks were needed to construct the strange particles. As unlikely as all this sounds, Gell-Mann received the Nobel Prize in Physics in 1969.

The quarks worked so well in explaining the particles under the influence of the strong force that it was natural to wonder if quarks were not something more than a convenient mathematical fiction. The first clues came in 1969 from an atom smasher at Stanford University in California. This device, called a linear accelerator, hurled electrons down a two-mile tube, deep into the nuclear interior. Electrons do not get bogged down in the strong forces holding the nucleus together. At the time, most scientists thought the electrons would be deflected by the positively charged protons. But just as Rutherford had been amazed when his alpha particles came bouncing back toward him, the Stanford experimenters were amazed when some of the elec-

The Stanford Linear Accelerator

trons ricocheted off the nucleus as if they had hit some minute, rock-hard particle. The deeply penetrating electrons had come upon the building blocks of protons and neutrons, which up to that time were thought to be the most elementary particles in the atomic nucleus. The quark had been found.

In 1974, just as most but not all physicists were beginning to feel satisfied with the three-component quark theory, a new particle, the *J-psi* particle, was discovered independently at two different laboratories. To account for the new particle, a new quark was needed; the *charmed* quark had already been named by Sheldon Glashow, another American physicist who had anticipated that it would be needed.

And then the whole process was repeated in 1977 when the *upsilon* particle was discovered. Now five quarks were needed: up, down, strange, charmed, and the new one—*bottom*. The upsilon is a bottom-quark–antiquark pair.

Recently another quark, the *top* quark, which symmetry considerations suggest should exist, has apparently been found, although the evidence is not completely conclusive. In any case, physicists are pretty well convinced that there are at least six different kinds, or "flavors" of quarks, as they are called.

All the particles made from quarks "feel" the strong force, but other particles, such as the electron and the neutrino, which appear to be basic particles like the quarks, do not interact with the strong force. The muon—the fat electron that was at first thought to be Yukawa's predicted exchange-force particle—is one of these that does not feel the strong force. Later an even heavier electron, the *tau* particle, was discovered. As the electron has a neutrino associated with it—as we noted with the breakup of a neutron into an electron, a proton, and a neutrino—so the muon has a neutrino associated with it, called a *muon neutrino*. No neutrino partner has yet been directly found for the tau particle, but everyone will be very much surprised if it does not exist.

All the basic particles not affected by the strong force are called *leptons*, after the Greek word meaning "swift ones." At present, it appears that all the basic particles of the universe are composed of six quarks and six leptons. And as far as anyone can tell, these particles are points in space with no internal structure.

Now that we have identified the basic building blocks of the universe, for the time being at least, we must complete the story by discussing the forces that interact with the basic particles. As we know, four such forces have been identified. One of these, the electromagnetic force is understood in terms of photons, which provide the vehicle by which electrons and other charged particles interact with each other. The strong nuclear force that held protons and neutrons together was first understood in terms of Yukawa's meson, the pion. But now that we know that protons and neutrons are made from quarks, we must look for a new particle—or particles—to hold the quarks together.

At present a theory called quantum chromodynamics predicts that the quarks are held together by eight different kinds of particles called *gluons*. The theory is called quantum *chromo*dynamics because each quark has associated with it three different kinds of interactions, which are named three different colors—say the primary colors, red, yellow, and blue. Of course this doesn't mean that the forces actually have these colors; it is simply a way to give the forces unambiguous names that fit with the general whimsy of the other names—quarks, flavor, gluons, up, down, charmed, strange—used in the new particle physics.

Quantum chromodynamics has come out of the gauge symmetry ideas that we discussed earlier. Although the details are very technical, the general idea is again that forces are needed to restore symmetry in nature. These symmetries, however, don't have to do with the spatial symmetries such as we met in General Relativity. There we needed the force of gravity to make all frames of reference equally valid. In quantum chromodynamics, the symmetries have to do with the properties of the particles themselves; they are called internal symmetries, and the quark colors are related to these internal symmetries.

According to a general principle of nature, certain identical particles, such as electrons, cannot occupy the same locale at the same time. This is a little like saying you can't put ten pounds of potatoes in a five-pound bag. In somewhat the same sense, just any three quarks can't be brought together to produce a proton; they must all be different colors if they are to occupy the same locale. Particles that can't occupy the same locale at the same time are called *fermions*, after Enrico Fermi, who proposed the neutrino.

Particles like photons, that *can* occupy the same locale at the same time, are called *bosons*, after the Indian physicist Satyendranath Bose, who worked on the statistics of subatomic particles. All of the exchange particles are bosons. We can think of bosons as being like waves in the sense that any number of waves can converge and occupy the same point in space.

The internal symmetry we spoke of refers to the fact that it shouldn't make any difference which quark, in the proton, is which color, as long as all three are different. In other words, we should be at liberty to change the colors around arbitrarily, just as we are at liberty, in General Relativity, to insist that the laws of nature should be the same for any observer whatever his frame of reference. In General Relativity, the gravitational force field was required to make all frames of reference equally valid. In quantum chromodynamics, the eight gluon exchange particles are necessary if we are to be at liberty to interchange the quark colors arbitrarily. This kind of arbitrary interchange symmetry is not the kind of thing we encounter in everyday life, but it expresses the idea that nature's law should not depend on how we decide to name the quarks in a proton, or any particle composed from quarks.

The gluon exchange forces are so effective that it appears in both experiment and theory that a quark cannot exist by itself; there is always at least a pair of quarks. If we direct great amounts of energy at a quark pair making up a meson, for example, we don't break the meson into two quarks; we just get more quarks. That is, the energy we are aiming at the meson is being used to create more quarks, according to the relation $E = mc^2$. The idea that quarks can't be

Fig. 8. Quarks may move around relatively freely in the bag but cannot break through.

separated is called confinement. A model that depicts confinement well is the bag model; here two or more quarks are inside a bag where they are relatively free to move around, but the bag is so strong that no quark can ever break out.

We need to add that quantum chromodynamics is not a mature theory like Special Relativity, and is still in the process of evaluation and development. There is still much to do, and ten years from now the theory may be a historical curiosity.

A theory for the weak force has also been developed out of the ideas of gauge symmetry, and this theory has had some startling successes. First it predicts that three particles should be involved in the weak force. Two of these, the W *particles*, are electrically charged with opposite polarities; and the third, the Z *particle*, is neutral and something like a heavy photon. These were discovered in 1984 by Carlo Rubbia and Simon van der Meer, as we said in Chapter 1. But even before this, in 1979, the prime developers of the theory of the weak force—Steven Weinberg, Sheldon Glashow, and Abdus Salam—were awarded a Nobel Prize because, although there was little experimental evidence at the time, the theory seemed complete and likely to succeed.

Like the photons and gluons, the three particles are another mechanism for generating exchange forces. Here again we can imagine two people throwing a beach ball back and forth. But for the electroweak forces, the beach ball is quite heavy, so the players must stand close together to keep the ball within each other's range. That is, the electroweak force has a much shorter range than the nuclear force.

We can understand this in terms of the energy-time uncertainty principle. Since the weak force particles, the W and Z particles, are heavy—that is, they are created at the expense of considerable energy—they cannot stray far away from home. But the photons, being massless, can stray as far from home as they like, which accounts for the fact that electromagnetic forces extend indefinitely.

Perhaps the most satisfying aspect of this new theory for weak interactions is that it also provides a home for the electromagnetic force. As has happened so often in the past, what seemed to be two forces was in fact different faces of the same force. This new marriage of the electromagnetic and the weak forces is called simply the electroweak force. And now we are back to three basic forces: gravity, the strong force, and the electroweak force. We shall have more to say about this in the next chapter.

Finally we need to consider the gravitational force. General Relativity depicts gravity in terms of the curvature of spacetime. But gravity, like the strong force and the electroweak force, can also be considered in terms of exchange forces. Here the force between two massive bodies is understood in terms of countless particles, called *gravitons*, flying back and forth between the bodies and providing the necessary interaction. Like photons, gravitons are massless, which accounts for the infinite reach of gravitation.

As we have mentioned before, there has been very little success in joining gravity with nature's other forces. But as we shall see in our final chapter, the attempt to meld all of nature's building blocks and forces is providing us with a glimpse of the very origin of the universe.

12

The Ultimate Free Lunch

SIR ARTHUR STANLEY EDDINGTON, born in 1882, was one of England's most prominent astronomers. His work provides a foundation for much of our understanding of the constitution of the sun and other stars. Eddington was best known to the general public for the expedition he led to Africa to observe the 1919 total eclipse of the sun. Einstein's General Theory of Relativity was only three years old at the time, and one of its predictions was that light would take a curved path as it passed near a massive body like the sun.

During a total eclipse it is possible to see stars whose light is ordinarily drowned out by the sun's light. Some of these stars are in nearly the same direction as the sun, so their light rays pass near the sun on their way to earth. If the rays are bent, the stars appear to be slightly displaced from their actual locations. General Relativity predicts the exact amount of this displacement (fig. 1). When Eddington announced the results of his measurements, the world was enthralled. Space *was* curved, and Einstein became famous.

In his later years, Eddington was fascinated with some of nature's numbers such as the speed of light, the age of the universe, and the number of atoms in the universe. He became convinced that a deep study of these numbers would be the key to understanding nature. Most scientists thought this work was little more than reading tea leaves, and one group of young scientists in England cooked up an elaborate joke at Eddington's expense:

In 1931 a bogus paper titled "Concerning the Quantum Theory of the Absolute Zero" appeared in a prestigious scientific journal. The paper concluded by saying that its whole premise was based on one of the numbers Eddington considered a cornerstone of his work. The paper had been so carefully prepared that the journal's editor was completely taken in by the hoax.

After the hoax was exposed, a tall, blond, twenty-seven-year-old Russian physicist, George Gamow, could not sleep for a week, according to his roommate at the Niels Bohr Institute for Theoretical Physics, in Copenhagen. Gamow, a great practical joker himself, had not been a part of the plot, and he was determined not to be left out again. Sometime later a legitimate paper written by Eddington, "Origin of Cosmic Penetration Radiation," appeared in the same journal. Gamow and a friend immediately wrote letters from different cities to the journal's editor, expressing sympathy that he had been hoaxed again and that another retraction would be required.

Gamow's contributions to science are many and varied. He was one of the first to explain radioactivity correctly by applying quantum mechanics to the nucleus of the atom, and he was a major contributor to decoding the DNA molecule, which determines individual heredity characteristics. He is also credited with coining the phrase "Big Bang"; if he did not coin the phrase, he certainly is the father of this modern version of the birth of the universe.

Although Gamow enjoyed playing a joke on Eddington, he shared Eddington's belief that much could be learned about the universe

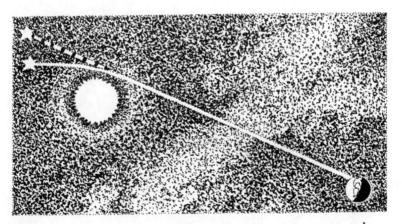

Fig. 1. Light is bent in a gravitational field so that a star appears to be displaced from its normal position.

by studying its basic particles. As we have said, General Relativity predicts that the universe is dynamic; and this, coupled with Hubble's discovery of the expanding universe, means that at some time the universe exploded from a point—the Big Bang.

Gamow began to think what the universe must have been like at time zero of the Big Bang. One thing was clear: the closer the approach to time zero, the hotter the universe must have been. The present temperature merely reflects the fact that the universe had been hotter earlier and has cooled to its present temperature as it expanded. At the billion-degree temperatures in the early universe, atoms would have been shaken apart, so we must conclude that today's atoms are simply fossils created from more basic components that could withstand the earlier high temperatures.

Before Hubble's discovery of the expanding universe, most scientists tried to understand the elements in it in terms of a universe that had always existed. With this assumption it seemed likely that most atoms were continually torn apart and reforged in the interior of the stars. Gamow realized that if there really had been a Big Bang,

George Gamow

the generally accepted account would not explain the composition of the universe. He proposed that the universe, moments after the Big Bang, consisted mainly of pure energy—*yelm* he called it, after the Greek word used in an early Greek version of Genesis to describe the chaos out of which the universe formed. As the universe began to expand and cool, he suggested, the pure energy, in the form of photons, coalesced into the elements we know today.

One prediction of this model, which was not particularly stressed at the time, was that the strong interaction between the newly forming elements and the photons would finally end at a sufficiently low temperature. Then the photons would become detached from the matter and expand with space. We can think of this flood of photons as a flash of electromagnetic energy that was released sometime after the Big Bang. If the theory was correct, then some much dimmer remnant of the flash should still be around. There was some talk of looking for this ancient light, but no serious steps were taken, partly because no one knew how to go about looking.

Gamow, with the help of a young scientist, Ralph Alpher, published his paper on April Fool's Day in 1948. Always the joker, Gamow couldn't resist adding the name of Nobel Prize-winning physicist Hans Bethe as a coauthor, so that the authors were Alpher, Bethe, and Gamow; it seemed fitting to Gamow that a paper on the origin of the universe should have authors whose names paralleled the first three letters of the Greek alphabet—alpha, beta, gamma; and Gamow knew that Bethe had been one of the authors of the bogus paper needling Eddington.

In 1965, two American scientists, Arno Penzias and Robert Wilson, testing a new dish antenna for satellite communications, noticed a strange, weak noise that wouldn't go away. No matter what they tried or in what direction they pointed their antenna, the noise was always there. After dismissing every conceivable possibility, they decided the low-level noise was coming from outer space. Consultation with other scientists confirmed their conclusion that the noise was the ancient light, now cooled to radio noise, predicted by Gamow. A relic from the very beginning of the universe had been found, and it had just the characteristics that later improvements of Gamow's work predicted. This discovery, ranking with Hubble's discovery of the expanding universe, won a Nobel Prize for Penzias and Wilson a few years after their discovery.

Approaching the end of this book, we also approach the frontiers of research and theorizing on the origin and nature of the universe. As with any frontier, there is much confusion and uncertainty. At present several theories are being proposed, compared, and studied. It is not possible to consider all of them here, but we can highlight the general directions of theoretical developments and leave history to discard the dead ends and focus on the successes.

As always, the goal of the theorists is to bring more and more of nature under fewer and fewer laws. In the last ten years, as we have seen, electromagnetism and the weak force have been merged into the electroweak force, with gauge symmetry pointing the way. And quantum chromodynamics, the theory of the strong force—again shaped by gauge symmetry principles—has successfully explained most of the particle interactions observed in the world's most powerful atom smashers. Quantum chromodynamics and the electroweak theory, together, are usually called the standard model, and with the standard model scientists have been able to trace the evolution of the universe back to about 10^{-12} seconds after time zero. The figure 10^{-12} means 1 divided by a 1 followed by twelve zeroes, which is a very, very tiny fraction of a second after time zero.

The theorists are well on their way toward bringing the strong force and the electroweak force into one theory. Again developed with the guidance of gauge symmetry, a number of approaches receiving active consideration are lumped together under the general heading "grand unified theories." Most of these theories predict that the proton, one of the stable building blocks of the universe, eventually decays into pure radiation. But the predicted process is incredibly slow, and no decays have been found to date. In spite of this difficulty, most theorists believe they are on the right track. If they are, it seems possible to trace the universe back to about 10^{-35} seconds after time zero. Before we pursue this possibility, let's consider, in general terms, the underlying themes of these unifying theories.

Let's imagine a checkerboard before the beginning of a game. The red checkers are on one side of the board, and the black checkers on the other. Here at the beginning we have complete symmetry: the rules are the same for both players, and the checkers are lined up symmetrically on both sides of the board. Later on, after the game has started, we see the checkers in a somewhat random pattern over the board.

Trying to understand the universe is somewhat like trying to figure out the checker game after it has gone on for a while. Here we are, about 15 billion years after the Big Bang—after the game has started—trying to figure out what is going on. We see the stars and other celestial objects dispersed throughout the universe in varying degrees of organization, and we see certain patterns in the laws and particles that make up the universe. But it is not at all obvious from what we see that complete symmetry rules the universe. Yet most theorists think that is the case.

Like a checker game governed by symmetrical rules with a symmetrical placement of the checkers at the beginning of the game, the universe does not necessarily evolve in a symmetrical way even though the laws that govern it are symmetrical. The patterns we see in the matter and laws of the universe today do not accurately reflect the underlying laws that ultimately govern. These laws have been hidden from us as the universe evolved, just as the initial symmetry of the checker game underway is hidden from us.

This belief in an underlying, hidden symmetry is another way of saying that all the laws of the universe eventually boil down to one law. Furthermore, the particles of the universe—the leptons, quarks, and exchange-force particles—should all be different manifestations of the same basic particles. And just as the underlying symmetry of a checker game becomes more apparent as we approach its beginning, so the basic symmetry of the universe becomes clearer as we approach its beginning.

We have two ways to look toward the early moments of the universe. One way, as we have seen, is using optical and radio telescopes that allow us to see back in time, to when the universe was hot and more compact. The other way is to recreate the conditions of the universe as they were near the beginning. This is the role of the atom smashers, in which we can momentarily produce the temperatures of the early universe. To date, with these machines we can generate temperatures that go back to the time when the universe was about 10^{-12} seconds old.

According to the standard model, this is just about the time the electromagnetic force and the weak force operate as one force. At this temperature, the underlying symmetry of the electromagnetic and the weak forces is not hidden as it is later by the evolution and cooling of the universe. And in fact it is just at these temperatures that we begin to see in atom smashers the W and Z particles predicted by the electroweak theory.

As we go back further in time, to even higher temperatures, we would expect to see the electroweak and strong forces join. According to the grand unified theories, this should happen when the universe was about 10^{-35} seconds old. Finally, when the universe is about 10^{-43} seconds old, the force of gravity should start to merge with the now-merged electroweak-strong force (fig. 2). In addition, as we approach the earliest fraction of a second after the Big Bang, the atoms break down into protons, neutrons, and so forth, which then break down into quarks, which along with the leptons and the exchange particles make up the universe.

But even before this, the individual identity of the quarks, leptons, and exchange particles is lost in the cauldron of the very beginning of the universe. The lost identity of the particles is somewhat like a handful of coins losing their head-or-tail identities if we shake them in a pan. As long as the pan is still, we can see the coins with their head or tail sides showing clearly. But if we shake the pan vigorously, the agitated movement of the coins blurs their identities so that it no longer makes sense to talk about a coin having two different sides.

Fig. 2. As the universe cools and expands, the basic forces separate.

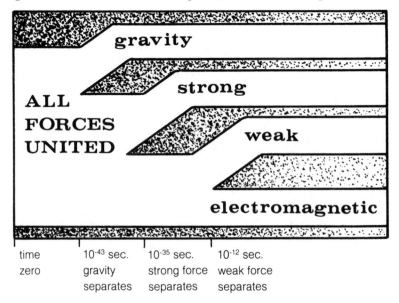

Even though bigger atom smashers are on the drawing boards, no one expects ever to be able to recreate the very earliest moments of the universe. For those times we must rely on ever-better optical and radio telescopes and more complete theories that will spell out in detail what we should observe about today's universe that was dictated by the details of the very earliest universe, just as the weak radio signals we find today were dictated by the Big Bang.

The general philosophy of theories about nature is that whatever is not forbidden is allowed, but with the laws of quantum mechanics, what is possible becomes restricted. And when we combine Special Relativity with quantum mechanics, what is allowed is even more restricted. The hope is that with a complete, unified theory of the laws of nature, everything will be determined.

We have seen an example of this process in action. When early experimenters measured the speed of light, they had no idea why they obtained the figure they did. Later, when Maxwell merged electricity and magnetism, his new theory not only predicted light waves but also gave the speed at which they travel. The speed of light was no longer an arbitrary figure. Today we have many quantities not determined by theory; they must be measured. These include the mass of the electron, the mass of the proton, and so on. So another ultimate goal is to form a unified theory that will determine all basic quantities, leaving nothing that needs to be measured and then inserted into the theory.

Now that we've learned something of the general goals of the theorists looking for the ultimate, unified theory, let's return to see what the grand unified theories, bringing together everything but gravitation, suggest to us about the evolution of the universe. As we said, these theories are by no means law, and what they suggest is subject to modification at any time. Successful as the Big Bang theory was, it left many unanswered questions.

We shall look at only one of them: Why is the universe, on the large scale, as smooth as it is? The grand unified theories suggest an answer. As we have seen, when Dirac merged quantum mechanics and Special Relativity, he got a surprising result: His equation predicted antimatter. When quantum chromodynamics and the electroweak theory are merged to produce a grand unified theory, another surprising result emerges: A mechanism for expanding the universe appears. The details are very technical, but the surprising result is that in the very early stages, between about 10^{-35} and 10^{-33} seconds from time

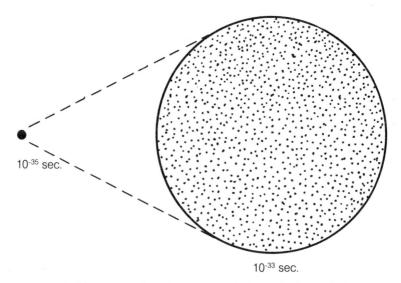

Fig. 3. The very early universe expanded rapidly for an instant.

zero, the universe underwent a dramatic expansion now called the inflationary period. The expansion during the inflationary period is related to the time when the strong force was becoming decoupled—or frozen out, as it is called—from the electroweak force.

We can think of this transition period as being something like what happens when ice melts. If we cool water in a freezer, its temperature drops steadily until the water begins to freeze. The temperature remains constant until the freezing is completed. Then the temperature begins to drop again. We can understand this if we realize that water and ice are made of the same kind of molecules. In ice the molecules are positioned in nearly motionless uniform arrays, like a platoon of soldiers standing at attention.

If we heat ice, its temperature slowly rises until it reaches the melting point. There the temperature remains constant until the ice is melted. This is because the heat is going into disrupting the uniform arrangement of the molecules. Once the disruption is completed, when the ice has melted, the temperature continues to rise.

It is often a feature of nature that any time there is a change from one state to another, heat is either absorbed or released. In the case of the evolution of the universe, the change in states corresponds to the period when the electroweak force and the strong force were separated, releasing heat in the process and causing the universe to expand dramatically. After the change was complete, the universe went back to expanding at the rate normally associated with the Big Bang.

It is the rapid inflation that accounts for the uniformity of the present universe. Just before the inflation, all parts of the universe visible to us were near each other, and so interacted to smooth out any gross nonconformities. During inflation, the universe expanded at a rate that exceeded the speed of light; space expanding at the

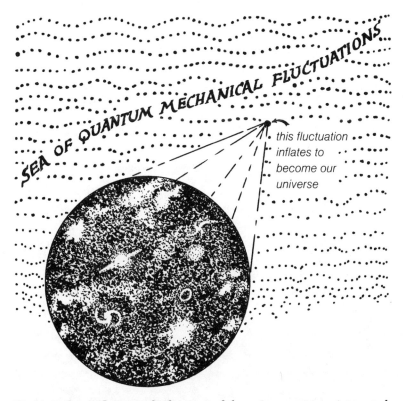

this fluctuation inflates to become our universe

Fig. 4. Before inflation, only the parts of the universe near us interacted to smooth out any gross nonconformities. Other parts of the universe, not visible to us, may have different distributions of galaxies.

speed of light does not violate Special Relativity because no energy movement is involved.

After inflation the expansion rate dropped to about its present value, and over the eons the parts of the universe that were once near us are coming into view again. More distant parts of the universe may have had distributions of matter different from the one we see, but these are so far away that their light has not yet reached us. So even though the universe may not have been uniformly smooth overall immediately after time zero, the part that we see is uniformly smooth.

We now come to the time before the inflationary period, when the strong-electroweak force was merged with gravity. The pieces of the universe are now crammed so close together that gravity cannot be ignored. There is no satisfactory theory for this today, although some ideas are on the horizon. In one idea the elementary particles of the universe are incredibly short threads of matter, less than one-trillionth the diameter of the proton, called *strings*. The string theory seems to do away with many of the singularities that plague most theories because the strings, having a finite size—unlike quarks, for example—do not cause the theory to blow up. The string theory also seems to have few quantities that need to be measured, and thus has one of the features we would expect from a theory that includes all the forces of nature. But it is much too early to say what the ultimate fate of the string theory will be. Perhaps some of the readers of this book will contribute to that answer.

We now move toward the very moment of the Big Bang. This near to time zero, it is not even clear what time means. As we have seen, gravity and spacetime are unalterably mixed when the universe curves in on itself, and we cannot imagine any more extreme curvature than the first instant after time zero, whatever that may mean. Nevertheless, not even these difficulties have stopped speculation.

To continue our story, we return to quantum mechanics and the energy-time principle. It was this principle, we recall, that allowed an electron, for example, to lend energy momentarily for the creation of a photon. But what if there is no electron, or other particle, to lend energy? Could particles appear out of nothing in a vacuum? According to theory and a good many experiments, the answer is yes.

Let's consider one possibility. Suppose an electron and its twin, a positron (made from antimatter) appear spontaneously in space. Since the electron has a negative charge and the positron a positive charge,

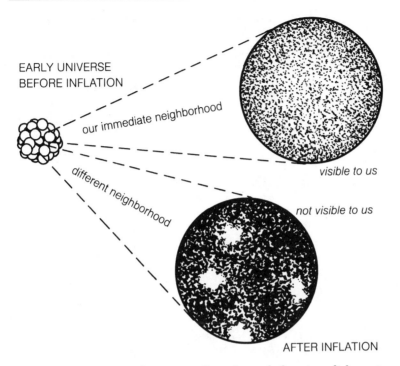

EARLY UNIVERSE
BEFORE INFLATION

our immediate neighborhood

different neighborhood

visible to us

not visible to us

AFTER INFLATION

Fig. 5. The universe may have grown from the seed of a primordial quantum mechanical fluctuation.

the net charge is zero. So at least where the charge is concerned, the net charge was zero before the particle pair appeared and is still zero after they appeared. In some sense, then, nothing new has been created. Further, if the particle pair do not last too long, their appearance does not violate the idea that energy—and thus mass—can not be either created or destroyed. Projection of this argument leads to the conclusion that a vacuum is really a vast sea of particles fluctuating in and out of existence.

Suppose now that the seed of the entire universe started as one of these quantum-mechanical fluctuations. Without inflation, the fluctuation would have soon disappeared back into the vacuum. But with inflation it has the chance to grow into a full-fledged universe. Whether the universe continues to expand or collapses depends, as we discussed earlier, on the amount of its mass. With enough mass the universe, under gravitational attraction, eventually collapses back on itself and disappears into the quantum mechanical "foam." With less mass the universe continues to expand forever, never coming under the dominance of gravitation. The most widely accepted version of the inflationary universe predicts that the total mass is just on the boundary between a collapsing universe and an expanding universe.

The observations to date indicate that the mass of the universe is only about ten percent or so of the amount required by the inflationary theory. But like the General Theory of Relativity, the inflationary theory is so attractive that many scientists believe that the missing mass will eventually be found.

There are many suggestions concerning the nature of the missing mass, but one widely held notion is that the mass is in the form of a particle yet to be discovered. Since the particle has not yet been seen, it must react very weakly with the particles of the universe we know about; it must also be massive to account for the necessary missing mass. This Weak-Interacting, Massive Particle has in fact already been dubbed the "WIMP," and the search for it is under way.

The inflationary theory does not appear to violate any of the basic laws of physics. It seems that the universe emerges from nothing. As American physicist Alan Guth, the originator of the inflationary theory, said, if this idea is correct, then "the universe is the ultimate free lunch." We have literally gotten, not just something, but everything from nothing.

Bizarre? Very. Ten or fifteen years ago no serious scientist would have even considered the subject of the origin of the universe. Yet today some of the most distinguished theorists of our time are pursuing it eagerly. Within the last five years, many of the major problems of the origin and evolution of the universe have been, if not resolved, at least thoroughly uncovered.

What good can come from study of the origin, evolution, and makeup of the universe? One of the most important results, certainly, is that it so greatly expands man's capacity for thinking about a world and a universe that is "real" but outside the realm of the visible and our ordinary way of looking at things. The very fact that ordinary human beings can speculate about galaxies billions of light years away, curved space, and string particles is amazing. That scientists from many different cultures and nations can formulate theories about these things, make predictions based on their theories, and build instruments to test their predictions is even more amazing.

This is an exciting time to be living on our planet Earth, in a universe filled with promises and puzzles. We have grown up thinking from our everyday experiences that we live in a material universe. Now scientists are telling us that this is not true. "Basically what we learned in grade school and high school about the definition of matter is wrong," says David Schramm, a University of Chicago astrophysicist. "We were taught that matter occupies space. That's not right. The fundamental building blocks of matter don't occupy space. What occupies space is the structure built up by the forces between particles."

Adjusting our perception of the universe to the new theories is even more challenging than the problems earlier people had with accepting a spherical earth in place of a flat one. Who knows what may result from our expanded concepts?

From a practical standpoint, even if some scientists are not driven by the search for a better mousetrap, it is clear that the fruits of their labors have led to better mousetraps. When Newton wondered why an apple falls toward the earth, he set in motion a chain of events that led to an understanding of the tides, to weather satellites, and to man landing on the moon. When Maxwell pondered the connection between electricity and magnetism, he paved the way for radio, television, and electronic photos of the moons of Jupiter. So where will black holes, quarks, and quasars lead us? Nobody knows. That's the fascination of our tour of the universe. We never know what may be around the next corner.

Glossary

Alpha particle—The nucleus of the helium atom.

Antimatter—A form of matter that, when it comes in contact with ordinary matter, combines to form pure radiation.

Atom—The smallest elementary particle that still retains the properties of an element.

Beta particle—An electron.

Big Bang—A theory of the creation of the universe that assumes that all matter, space, and time expanded from a beginning compact state of enormous density.

Black hole—A massive body, such as a star, which has gravitationally collapsed upon itself to form a "knot" in space-time from which nothing, including light, can escape.

Bosons—The forces carrying particles such as the photon, the pion, and the gluon. Bosons can occupy the same space at the same time.

Color—One of the properties of quarks. It has nothing to do with ordinary color.

Eightfold way—A forerunner of the quark model of elementary particles.

Electromagnetic waves—Waves traveling at the speed of light in a vacuum resulting from the interaction of electric and magnetic fields.

Electron—The least massive elementary particle that carries an electric charge.

Element—A substance that cannot be broken down into any simpler substance without changing its nucleus.

Ether—An invisible substance once presumed necessary to account for gravitational interactions and the transmission of light.

Exchange particles—Particles that carry the fundamental forces.

Fermions—Elementary particles that cannot occupy the same space at the same time, in contrast to bosons. Protons and neutrons are fermions.

Gamma rays—Very energetic electromagnetic waves.

Gauge invariance—A characteristic of many physical theories that corresponds to the idea that the laws of nature should not depend on how we define the various components making up the theory.

Geodesic—The path taken by a light ray, which amounts to taking the shortest path.

Gluons—Carriers of the strong force between quarks.

Grand unified theories—Theories which unify the nuclear, weak, and electromagnetic forces into various aspects of the same force. The force of gravity is not included.

Leptons—Elementary particles that are not influenced by the strong force. The electron is an example.

Light year—The distance traveled by light in one year.

Mass—A property of matter that accounts for its resisting a change in motion. The weight of a chunk of matter is not the same as its mass. Weight depends on the strength of the gravitational force it experiences. For example, the weight of an apple on the moon is less than it is on the earth, but the mass is the same in both places.

Mesons—Elementary particles affected by the strong force.

Molecule—A combination of two or more atoms to form a substance with characteristics differing from those of the parent atoms. Combining sodium and chlorine atoms to form molecules of salt is an example.

Neutron—An elementary particle with zero charge which at one time was thought to be one of nature's basic building blocks.

Nucleus—The center or core of an atom, consisting of protons and neutrons.

Ockham's razor—A guiding principle in the formulation of nature's laws which says that one should always look for the simplest theory that explains the observations.

Photon—An elementary particle having zero mass and no electric charge.

Positrons—The antimatter form of electrons.

Proton—An elementary particle with a positive charge, which at one time was thought to be one of nature's basic building blocks.

Quantum mechanics—The basic theory of the microworld that reveals both the wave and particle nature of matter.

Quarks—The particles presently thought to be the basic building blocks of nature.

Quasars—Astronomical objects that appear to be starlike but that radiate energy greatly exceeding the energy radiated by any single star.

Singularity—A region where the laws of physics break down.

Spacetime—In Newton's era, space and time were thought to be independent, but Einstein's Special Theory of Relativity unifies space and time into one whole called spacetime.

Strong force—Nature's strongest basic force, responsible for holding the atom's nucleus together.

Symmetry—The observation, as well as the belief, that the laws of nature are balanced much as the two wings of a butterfly are balanced and symmetrical.

Uncertainty principle—A result of quantum mechanics which says that it is impossible to know both the position and velocity of a particle at the same time.

Weak force—One of nature's basic forces responsible for the transformations of atoms. Radioactive decay of uranium into lead is an example.

Index

PHOTO CREDITS

$16.95

DATE			

© THE BAKER & TAYLOR CO.